LEARN TO LOVE YOURSELF ENOUGH

Seven steps to improving your self-esteem and your relationships

ANDREW G. MARSHALL

BLOOMSBURY

LONDON · BERLIN · NEW YORK · SYDNEY

To Natalie Hunt

*Thanks for your thought-provoking questions
and eye for detail.*

First published in Great Britain 2011

Some of this material has appeared in a different context in
The Single Trap, published by Bloomsbury

Bloomsbury Publishing Plc
36 Soho Square
London W1D 3QY

Bloomsbury Publishing, London, New York and Berlin

A CIP catalogue record for this book is
available from the British Library

ISBN 978 1 4088 0261 8

10 9 8 7 6 5 4 3 2 1

Typeset by Hewer Text UK Ltd, Edinburgh
Printed in Great Britain by Clays Limited, St Ives Plc

www.bloomsbury.com/andrewgmarshall

Seven steps to improving
your self-esteem
and your relationships

INTRODUCTION

Seven Steps is a series of books offering straight-forward advice for creating successful and fulfilling relationships. Getting the most out of love needs skills and the good news is that these skills can be learned.

If there is a critical voice in your head which not only runs you down but also makes it hard to accept praise from work colleagues, friends or family, this book will help you make peace with yourself and the world around you. Unlike many programmes for boosting self-esteem, I will not just treat the symptoms but go to the root causes of your negative messages and show you how to deal with the past. In this way, you will not only learn how to challenge that little negative voice in your head, but also how to replace it with some-thing kinder, more understanding and loving. Most importantly, by improving your relationship with yourself, you will improve all your relation-ships – so that if you're looking for love, you will start attracting people who'll treat you better (rather than play games), and if you're in a loving relationship, it will become more equal and balanced.

In devising this programme, I have drawn on twenty-five years' experience as a marital therapist. However, I have changed names, details and sometimes merged two or three of my clients' stories to protect their identity and confidentiality.

Andrew G. Marshall
www.andrewgmarshall.com

STEP

UNDERSTAND
THE PROBLEM

It is a common piece of advice – you've heard it a million times on television talk shows and from friends and family: 'You've got to love yourself before you can love anybody else.' There are also variations on this theme, such as: 'If you don't hold yourself in high regard, nobody else will' and 'Loving yourself is the greatest love of all.' In fact, we've heard this basic idea packaged in so many ways, so many times, that we tend to switch off and carry on as normal. But what would our lives be like if we did at least *like* ourselves? Wouldn't everything be easier, and certainly more enjoyable, if we weren't so self-critical? We'd start standing up for ourselves and stop friends or work colleagues taking advantage of us. When looking for love, we'd make better choices or, when we'd found a partner, we'd not let him or her walk all over us. Unlike a lot of other obvious truths, there is a real nugget of wisdom in the idea of loving ourselves. So why haven't we taken the advice on board?

From time to time, I meet people who seem to have a very high opinion of themselves. 'I'm only attracted to really handsome men,' said Charlotte, forty-two, when she arrived in my counselling office. 'Unfortunately, they've all known just how gorgeous they were.' As I took down her relationship history, Charlotte peppered her conversations with examples of just how much she loved herself: 'I'm used to a lot of attention', or had been loved: 'He absolutely adored me and would have done anything for me.'

Twenty-five years of counselling has taught me that how something appears on the surface is often very different to the reality underneath. At first sight, Charlotte did seem confident and up-front. However, she felt a little brittle, as if with the slightest setback or anything less than 100 per cent approval she would start to crumble. She had come into counselling because, despite being able to attract plenty of men, she could not keep any she truly wanted (and did not seem to want the ones who wanted her). The more I got to know Charlotte, the more I realised that she was swinging from high to low self-esteem – with nothing much in the middle.

The effects of low self-esteem are all too evident in my counselling office. Jessica, thirty-four, wanted a long-term boyfriend but most of her relationships never seemed to go anywhere. She sighed heavily and looked down at the floor. 'I'm a complete failure with men. I'll meet these guys at parties and we'll click but somehow the relationships always end with me crying.' So I asked about her most recent boyfriend, Bob. 'I suppose I should have known better. That first night, when we were back at my flat, sitting on the sofa with a glass of wine, he said, "Are you sure you want to do this?" He'd even told me he was not looking for a relationship. But I didn't want him to go. Well, the inevitable happened and we made love. It was good and I developed feelings for him.' In effect, she had known that they were after different things: he was looking for casual sex and she wanted love. However, as she did not treat herself with respect, Bob probably felt that he had the green light to do the same. After half a dozen encounters, he became less and less available and eventually disappeared altogether.

Loving Yourself Enough

This concept comes from childcare, where experts have always known that if a baby is neglected, he or she will not only fail to thrive but also grow into a troubled and unhappy adult. Holding the destiny of your baby literally in your arms is a huge responsibility. Many new mothers feel overwhelmed and worry that anything less than perfection will cause lasting damage.

Fortunately, in the fifties, Donald Winnicott (an English paediatrician and psychologist) coined the term *good enough mother*. This mother provides enough care for her baby to prosper but, unlike the 'perfect' mother, does not provide everything that her child wants immediately, on demand, round the clock. Winnicott believed that if, by some miracle, we fulfilled every one of our children's needs, they would not develop properly and would find it difficult to grow into self-sufficient adults. In effect, small but manageable amounts of adversity provide important lessons for children. To modern minds, *good enough* is often seen as not good enough. We aim to do the very best for our children and then a little bit more. However, Winnicott would argue that we are not only driving ourselves mad but also failing our children.

So how does the *good enough* concept work with self-esteem? Unlike a lot of programmes, I will not be trying to boost you up with lots of self-improving statements or asking you to visualise the ideal outcome. To my mind, this is like trying to be a 'perfect' person and makes someone – like Charlotte – swing between loving themselves too much (and walking over everybody else) and hating themselves – like Jessica – for failing to achieve goals (and probably ending up being taken advantage of by others). Instead, my goal is to teach you to love yourself enough: enough to have love to offer others; enough to be open to receive love from others.

Before outlining my programme, I'd like you to take stock and access your feelings about yourself.

HOW GOOD IS YOUR SELF-ESTEEM?

With how many of the following statements do you agree?

	Sometimes	Often	Hardly ever
I stay in my comfort zone	☐	☐	☐
I get easily upset by criticism	☐	☐	☐
I feel the need to control situations	☐	☐	☐
I find it difficult to be open and honest with people	☐	☐	☐
I punish myself or blame others for my misfortunes	☐	☐	☐
There are times when I don't like myself	☐	☐	☐
I compare myself unfavourably with others	☐	☐	☐
I make myself feel better at the expense of others	☐	☐	☐
I feel alone and unprotected	☐	☐	☐
If I allow people to get close they won't really like me	☐	☐	☐

Scoring:

If you agree with a statement 'sometimes', score one point. If you agree 'often', score two points. If the answer is 'hardly ever', you score nothing. Total up your score and read the relevant section below.

Twelve and over: Everybody suffers from self-doubt from time to time – although some people are better at hiding it than others. Unfortunately, you have a low opinion of yourself and spend a lot of your time walking a tightrope between getting by and disaster. While your colleagues, family, friends or partner might shrug off a barbed comment, you spend hours analysing what was said, why, and castigating yourself for not doing better. However, take heart. My programme will help you understand the reasons for your low self-esteem, combat the negative voices in your head and help you begin to love yourself enough.

Less than twelve: Most of the time, you feel OK about yourself but your self-belief has been rocked by some recent catastrophe. Perhaps your partner is having an affair or has fallen out of love with you; maybe you lost your job or a rival was promoted over your head. Although perceived failure in one area can have a knock-on effect in others, the climb back will be more straightforward because you are building on fundamentally solid ground.

Examine Your Relationship With Your Parents

Low self-esteem is hard to combat because the roots stretch right back to our childhood. When we arrive in the world, our parents are normally the first people we meet, and how they respond to us provides important clues to our identity and how acceptable we are. Unfortunately, parents can give negative as well as positive feedback and because we are young, inexperienced and have no way of testing whether something is true or not, we believe everything we're told. Before long, the messages from our parents and caregivers are not just their opinions, prejudices and reflections of their own fallibility – but who we are.

Legacies from Fathers

A man's style of fathering is particularly significant for his daughters – because he is literally the first man in their lives – but it is also important for his sons, who learn about being a man from his example. There are six common types and although many men will use more than one, most have a core style – especially when they are tired or stressed out. With each type of fathering, there is an explanation of why this can lead to a poor self-image and a breakthrough tip, because improving your relationship with your father will improve your relationship with yourself.

Dictatorial

Many men still like to be head of the family, but there is a fine line between being in charge and dictatorial. Dictatorial fathers keep their sons' and daughters' noses to the school grindstone, and bedtimes, friends and chores can easily turn into a battleground. 'He once called me a slut because I wouldn't get out of bed at half past seven in the morning,' says Sian, a twenty-nine-year-old lawyer. 'His favourite phrase was "many a fortune has been made or lost before half past seven". He would even put a cold flannel on my face to get me up.' It was not just lounging around in a dressing gown that would set him off. 'I'd have to line up every-thing neatly on my dressing table and if I wanted to please him, I would rush around and do all that, but as soon as he was gone I'd take great pleasure in scruffing it all up again.' Dictatorial fathers want the best for their sons and daughters; although their form of tough love can push their children to the top of the class, it can also come across as deeply critical. What's more, these fathers can get so much under their sons' and daughters' skin that the children often end up not knowing their own mind.

Reasons why this can cause low self-esteem: Dictatorial fathers give their children a very distorted picture of themselves. They have such strong opinions that anybody else – who might provide a more balanced or alternative picture – is shouted down. This is why many children of dictatorial fathers come to conclusions about themselves based on little evidence – normally just one or two examples that are elevated to the general rule.

Breakthrough tip: Next time you are faced with a decision, ask yourself three questions. First, 'What would my father want me to do?' Second, 'What would I do if I was rebelling?' Just doing the opposite of what he would have wanted is not freedom either. Finally, ask, 'What would I like to do?'

Distant

Traditionally, men have been expected to keep their feelings tightly under control. So many grow up unaware or embarrassed about their emotions. When under stress, these men hide behind their newspaper, watch television, or lose themselves in some project in the garden. Whatever the shut-down strategy, these fathers remain a mystery to their children. Other fathers become distant through divorce or because their job takes them away.

'When Dad got home, if he was in a good mood or Mum reported good school grades, he might ruffle our hair, but it was never for more than a few seconds. Perhaps there is a statutory EU minimum for hair ruffling, which he was determined not to contravene,' says Belinda, forty-six. 'I often wished I'd knocked on his study door and had him explain his complicated filing system – everything had a place and mine was on the other side of that door. He's never told me he loves me; I guess he thinks I know.'

The daughters of distant fathers are drawn either to men who find it hard to commit or to men who keep their feelings to themselves. 'I've always felt happier when there was at least one time zone between me and my lover,' admits Belinda. Unfortunately, some daughters find themselves attracted to men who are so distant that they find it hard to commit to a relationship.

For men who are distant – like their fathers – it is often easier to make relationships, as many women enjoy drawing out their partners and explaining their emotions to them.

Reasons why this can cause low self-esteem: Although as an adult you might understand why your father was distant, as a child it will have felt deeply personal. This can leave you worried that nobody will ever truly love you. Even children of distant fathers who do get married wonder if they are worthy and, because they expect rejection, will sometimes assume the worst.

Breakthrough tip: Concentrate on changing something specific about your father's behaviour – for example, paying you more attention – rather than reeling off a list of complaints, which will probably make him retreat even further into himself. Next, narrow this request down into something as specific as possible. For example, talking to you when you phone the house. Finally, frame it as something positive about the future rather than as an accusation about the past. For example: when he answers the phone, suggest chatting for a while before he passes you on to your mother.

Destructive

These fathers cause harm because they have abandoned their daughters and sons or because they are not aware how thoughtless comments can ruin self-esteem.

'My dad is over six foot three and like a bull in a china shop; he opens his mouth first and thinks later,' says Tara, twenty-six. 'When I was about twelve and beginning to develop curves he caught me taking a tub of ice cream out of the freezer. "We'll have to watch out or you'll put on so much weight that none of the boys will fancy you," he told me. I should have clocked him, and to this day he still denies having said it, but I can trace my weight battles back to that solitary moment. Thinking of my first diet, which I pored over in one of my mother's magazines, the tinfoil packets of carrot sticks and the dry tuna that I used to take to school, makes me want to weep.'

These daughters often choose unavailable men – such as married ones – who will end up abandoning them and reconfirming their lack of self-worth. 'In my teens I was anybody's for a compliment,' says Tara. 'I slept with so many boys I got a reputation, but for those few moments I could pretend they cared. These days I'm wiser but I often take something as critical, even when it's not intended to be. When it's cold my boyfriend will say something innocent, like: "Don't you think you need a scarf?", but I will react as if he had said: "Your dress is too short and too small." I end up biting his head off all the time – not the most attractive quality.'

Reasons why this can cause low self-esteem: Experience has taught you that those closest to you are most likely to hurt you. This has left you with a toxic combination of fear of commitment and no confidence. In addition, you will often wrongly decide that you've made a fool of yourself or let yourself down.

Breakthrough tip: New Age philosophies talk about being positive but all that happens is that we give ourselves a hard time for not pulling off this trick. So try the opposite approach and listen to the critical voice. Once you have heard all it has to say, challenge the exaggerations and distortions. Finally, think: 'I can do things that are wrong but it is useful to look back, reflect and learn.' This balanced approach ultimately will make it easier for you to hear the positive.

Dangerous

These fathers never really grew up. They can be glamorous, exciting and terribly fascinating, but often there is a darker side: some are serial love cheats or have clocked up several wives, while others are dangerous because of drink or drugs. One thing is for sure: these men turn everything into a drama.

'Whenever my friends used to come round, Daddy had to be the centre of attention. He used to disappear upstairs and change into his genuine American Civil War uniform and then strut around the house showing off,' says Beverley, thirty-eight. 'It used to drive my mother up the wall, but I thought it was funny. When I became a teenager, I realised just how much his performance was fuelled by drink. Finally, I understood why he was always so over-emotional.'

Beverley has been dating unpredictable men ever since. 'I just don't seem to be able to avoid a challenge. My first boyfriend was the local life-guard and I was completely captivated by him. He'd be forever standing me up, but the worse he treated me the more I loved him. I thought his moodiness was because he was "strong and silent" but later I caught him in bed with another man.'

Unfortunately, the children of addicts are more at risk of developing an addiction problem themselves than the general population. For daughters of dangerous fathers, it is not just alcohol and drugs that can provide a buzz – difficult men can also be very addictive. The risk for the sons is imitating their father.

Reasons why this can cause low self-esteem: You are attracted to people who nearly always turn out to be bad for you and this has undermined your confidence in your own judgement. Worse still, your 'dangerous' lovers end up reinforcing the old messages from your childhood and make it even harder to believe in yourself.

Breakthrough tip: It is easy to be angry with these fathers – and you probably have every right to be – however, this just keeps the two of you stuck in the past. Instead, take a fresh look at both of you. Is his conduct still as bad? Could it be that you are trying to punish him? If so, who is really being harmed by this behaviour?

Doting

Everybody would like a father who dotes on them and, certainly, a daughter who grows up feeling adored will have more self-confidence. However, there can be a point where doting turns into spoiling.

'While Mummy sat on the back seat of the car, I rode up front with Daddy and I always got to choose where we stopped to eat. While I could have anything on the menu, as long as I enjoyed it, Mummy used to have the cheap things – like a bowl of soup. I'd scoff my way through the menu and eat something terribly exotic for pudding like rum baba,' says Kate, thirty-one.

However, it is hard to truly grow up if your doting father is always ready to ride to the rescue. Worse still, these women expect every man to treat them like a princess.

'My live-in boyfriend used to bring me biscuits and tea in bed and the whole weekend would revolve round my cravings,' admits Kate. 'But I became so bored that I started having a wild affair with someone who'd just got out of prison and used to clean his gun in bed. I'd never met anybody like him before. Not only could he not read or write, but he was also so unoriginal that he couldn't think of a name for his puppy, so he called it "dog". I couldn't talk to him, but who needs to talk! Yet, I would have died if Daddy had found out I even knew him.'

Dads are less likely to dote on boys, and therefore less likely to treat their sons as children, even after they have grown up. However, if a son's bad behaviour is not challenged – because Dad thinks he can do no wrong – he, too, can grow up to be selfish and unable to see anyone else's point of view.

Reasons why this can cause low self-esteem: The sons and daughters of doting fathers should be supremely confident. After all, they have been praised to the skies since birth. So what goes wrong? They are not allowed to fail (it is always someone else's fault), and without stumbling and falling, it is impossible to learn anything important. So there is always a gap between expectation and delivery; deep down, the sons and daughters know that they are not geniuses, but the drop to everyday normality seems immense.

Breakthrough tip: If you behave like a child, everybody else will slot into parent mode. So next time you are tempted to sulk, throw a tantrum or wheedle – very childish reactions – stop and ask yourself: What would an adult do?

Decent

These fathers provide a safe haven for their daughters to experiment in dealing with the opposite sex and they provide a good role model for their sons. Unlike doting fathers, they know when to draw the line and not let their children get too much of their own way.

'Whenever I or my sister had a problem, we always knew that we could go to Dad,' explains Adrienne, twenty-eight. 'He made us feel he was on our side but he would also make us realise that there was probably another side too. Sometimes he was busy, yet he seemed to know when it was something truly serious and he'd stop what he was doing.'

A lot of men grow into being decent fathers, and have a better relationship with their sons and daughters as adults than they had with them as children. This is partly because they have mellowed with age and partly because they are not so focused on their careers. It also helps that reaching adulthood gives us the chance to forge a more equal relationship with our parents. This type of father is also becoming more common as today's dads expect to have a more hands-on approach to being a parent. The impact on the children of decent fathers is generally positive and they grow up to be well-rounded and caring people.

Reasons why this can cause low self-esteem: If you have a decent father, it is likely that you have lost confidence as the result of a particular crisis – such as losing your job – rather than because of your upbringing. However, some decent fathers are so nice, considerate and ready to understand everyone's point of view that they do not stand up to other people – normally their wife – when their behaviour undermines their children's confidence. There is a second problem for the sons of decent fathers: you can grow up to be so decent yourself that women prefer you as a best friend rather than as a lover. This is particularly hard when you have to watch their hearts broken by yet another bad boy.

Breakthrough tip: It can be as harmful to have a totally positive picture of someone as to have a totally negative one. This is because life seldom comes in black and white but in shades of grey. So try and remember times when your father revealed feet of clay and discover a more balanced picture of him.

Legacies from Mothers

We all want our mother to be pleased with our achievements, partly because we know it makes her happy but mainly because it confirms that she has been a good mother. What's more, if she approves of our life, we feel worthy of her love. For all these reasons, it is harder to be dispassionate about our relationship with our mother than with our father, but a closer look can really help us understand the past and make better choices in the future.

There are six types of 'problem mothering', and for each there is advice on how to cope with the fallout and a breakthrough tip because, once again, a better relationship with your mother promotes a better relationship with yourself.

Martyr

Some women have good reason to complain. Life has dealt them a tough hand, for example, illness, desertion or destitution. Others have not had the opportunity to do what they wished. Before feminism became mainstream, talented women gave up their jobs and resented being stuck in the kitchen. Whatever the reason for their sacrifices, these mothers will not let anybody forget it and use guilt as a weapon. Worse still, their sons – and, in particular, their daughters – end up feeling responsible for their good days and bad days.

'I always end up getting edgy if anybody is upset and immediately want to be the peace-maker,' says twenty-eight-year-old Cathy. 'At work I find myself taking the blame for something being late – even if it landed on my desk only a couple of hours before the deadline.' Not surprisingly, Cathy found it hard to ask for what she needed. 'I couldn't just tell my partner I would have appreciated it if he arranged a birthday party for me at a local restaurant,' she confessed. 'Instead, I would drop hints and make suggestions and then get very angry when he didn't do anything.'

Reasons why this can cause low self-esteem: Your experiences of close relationships have been draining and claustrophobic. Your expectations of how something will turn out are also very negative. This makes you likely to overstate the likelihood of something going wrong and exaggerate the consequences of failure too. In your mind, you are always on the verge of being sacked, dumped or destroyed. In reality, you are late with a deadline (which can probably be extended) or your partner is angry about something (but will get over it) and you can always pick yourself up and start all over again.

Breakthrough tip: Understanding your mother's vulnerability is the first step to liberating yourself. Instead of getting angry, which will make her needier and perpetuate a vicious circle, tell her you love her and then laugh together when she goes over the top.

Critical

Mothers want the best for their children, but sometimes their desire for their sons and daughters to succeed comes across as criticism. Their children will often feel that they can never truly please them.

'I have become very critical of myself,' admits Richard, a thirty-three-year-old lawyer. 'It is almost as if I can hear her voice in my head pushing me on. On the one hand this has helped my career, but on the other, I never seem to enjoy my achievements.' Last Christmas, Richard talked to his aunt and got a wholly different take on his mother. 'She had bored her sister silly with all this praise and boasting about me. I just wish Mum had told *me*.'

Richard has had a very up-and-down relationship with his girlfriend. 'I find myself getting defensive about the slightest comment,' he admits. 'I took her to a Proms concert but she didn't seem to be enjoying it. In the interval, she commented that the conductor had taken a piece too fast. I started sulking; I'd gone to a lot of trouble getting those tickets.'

Reasons why this can cause low self-esteem: You either keep finding fault or you have become incredibly defensive, fly off the handle at the slightest thing and your partner feels that you are 'too high maintenance'. You are also likely to be hypersensitive and hear criticism even when none was intended.

Breakthrough tip: If critical mothering sounds familiar, try asking your mother's friends and other family members what she really thinks about you. Your mother probably assumes you already know her feelings or maybe fears praise will undermine your desire to achieve. Next time you overreact to something, stop and ask yourself if your mother's voice is mixed in there somewhere. If you have a tendency to become critical yourself, examine your standards and ask yourself how many are your own and how many are your mother's.

Perfect

Women put a lot of energy into being as good a mum as possible, but, for some, 'good' is never enough. They have to be super-mum: able to bake, hold down a job and still help out behind the scenes at the school play. Sons can idolise this type of mother to such an extent that other women have a tough job matching up to her. These men can also put potential partners on a pedestal and have 'polite' sex rather than allowing their women to be truly passionate. Meanwhile, the daughters of super-mums can find the legacy equally difficult. Tina, forty-two, started mothering her first husband: 'I felt like I had three children sometimes and, with no support, I ran out of energy. I wanted an equal partner.'

Reasons why this can cause low self-esteem: For women, you attract the sort of men that need their problems sorting out. Although this is flattering, it is not the foundation for a successful long-term relationship. For men, your expectations can be too high and this makes you easily disappointed. The other danger, for both the daughters and sons of perfect mothers, is to have incredibly high standards yourself so that anything short of perfection is viewed as failure. With this mindset, a five-star rave review, with one minor qualification, will be heard as a disaster.

Breakthrough tip: For daughters of perfect mothers, if you find yourself behaving like everybody's mother, step back and stop taking responsibility. For example, if you have to nag your partner to get up in the morning, remind him once and then leave it. He might be late for an appointment but he is an adult and accountable for his own choices. For sons of perfect mothers, think about the disadvantages of being so close to your mother. How much does she interfere in your life? Does she have strong views about your girlfriends? Compare your relationship with those of your friends; how does your mother demand more than their mothers? How do you feel about that?

Controlling

Another common example of great mothering that can turn into a problem is the over-attentive mum. It is a short step between looking out for your kids and smothering them; these 'takeover' mums seldom understand the difference.

'She was always ready to fight my battles at school by "having a word" with my teacher or the parents of another kid,' says Barry, thirty-four. 'At homework time, she seemed to be forever peering over my shoulder. She was great, but sometimes I felt swamped. Even to this day, I find it hard to let people get close for fear of them taking over.'

These mums are very likely to have strong opinions about their children's partners or lack of them. 'I had been dating Nicola for about six months,' says Michael, who is thirty years old, 'and Mum had told me that if I ever married she hoped it would be someone just like Nicola. I took this as maternal approval and even considered asking for Nicola's hand. Ultimately, I decided to trust my own judgement and to wait and see.' Mothers who feel confident and secure in themselves do not need to control their adult children.

Reasons why this can cause low self-esteem: Your biggest fear is being 'swallowed up' and losing control. You find yourself drawn to people who are, in some way, unavailable. They might live a long way away or are still emotionally tied to an ex-partner or too preoccupied with their work. If you are in a relationship, you will believe the only way to be lovable is to go along with all your partner's wishes. The result is not only a loss of confidence but also, at some profound level, being unsure of who you are and what you truly want from life.

Breakthrough tip: Your mother might be controlling because she really enjoys being a parent and finds it hard to let go – even though you've long since grown up. So try helping her find new interests. Explain what you find helpful and what is intrusive, and firmly police the difference. Although capitulating might seem easier in the short term, it could encourage your mother to become more controlling in the long term.

Frightened

Many mothers try and hide the effects of their husbands' drinking, gambling or violence. They want to protect their children but end up pulling them into the secret. If they are drinking themselves, or have a mental health problem, these mothers, sadly, provide very erratic childcare.

'There was this terrible secret in our family,' says Paula, who is now fifty. 'Although I didn't discover it until I was fifteen, I always knew we were different but couldn't put my finger on it. My grandmother had committed suicide but my mother never told me. Even now, I don't really understand why she fought so hard to keep it from me.'

Paula's upbringing has left her wary of being rejected. 'If I think there is the slightest danger of being dumped, I try and get in first,' she admits. 'I almost ended one promising relationship because this boyfriend hadn't phoned for several days. My mind came up with all sorts of possibilities, mainly centring around another woman. Before too long, I could see the two of them in the pub laughing at me. Finally, I left a nasty message on his machine. Later, I discovered his mother had been rushed to hospital.'

Reasons why this can cause low self-esteem: For daughters, the risk is that you too will grow up fearful of getting hurt and therefore holding men at arm's length. You can also feel responsible, like your mother, for managing everyone's behaviour. This is not only impossible but also sets you up for low self-esteem.

The sons of frightened mothers often become rescuers, which can be appealing to women. However, I do counsel men who are trying to fix women with chaotic lives or who are unable to commit. Alternatively, they can lose interest in a woman once her problems have been solved.

Finally, both the sons and daughters of frightened mothers can underestimate their abilities to deal with adversity.

Breakthrough tip: If your relationship with your mother has left you with the tendency to overreact, get some distance by imagining what a cool-headed friend might think of your interpretation. Be patient with yourself and do not expect too much too soon, as a difficult relationship with a mother is tougher to overcome than a difficult one with a father.

Racy

Sometimes a mother will try and compete with her daughter and even set herself up as a love rival.

'I often feel under the shadow of my mother,' says Jasmine, who is twenty-six. 'My boyfriends always get on very well with her but I think she laughs too loudly and shows too much cleavage. When I want just a bit of TLC, she is much more likely to give me sisterly advice like "Dust yourself off and get on with it". OK, she is quite cool and doesn't mind me bringing my boyfriends back home, but I never feel comfortable. One night, she brought this man home whom she'd picked up at a club and they had noisy sex that kept my boyfriend and me awake.'

For both sons and daughters, the risk is that there is a precocious interest in sex.

Reasons why this can cause low self-esteem: Daughters of racy mothers can often feel dowdy in comparison or, because their mothers rate sex appeal over everything else, discount their achievements in other areas. With this mindset, a great career or wonderful children become worthless. There is another problem. If all your self-worth hangs on success with men, any rejection is incredibly personal. The break-up is never caused by the man's failings but because you were not 'good enough' to keep him.

Breakthrough tip: This type of mothering has a greater impact on daughters, who take the competition personally, than on sons, who are just embarrassed. If these problems go back to your childhood, try forgiving your mother. It does not mean sanctioning what she did, but it will free you to start an adult relationship with her. For daughters, if the two of you are in competition today, remember it takes two to compete. If you refuse to enter, there is no race. For sons, ask about her relationship with her own mother and the morals of that time. Understanding how attitudes are handed from one generation to another and why your mother behaves as she does will help remove any lingering blame.

UNDERSTANDING YOUR PERSONAL LEGACY

Our parents' relationship sets the tone for our own relationships. Even if we want to be nothing like them, they remain a huge influence. The following exercise will help you understand the links.

1. Thinking about your childhood, write down your key thoughts about the following questions:

- Who made important long-term decisions in your household?
- Who challenged these decisions?
- Who made the day-to-day decisions?
- How were arguments settled?
- What happened when someone got angry?
- If you had a problem, to whom would you take it? Why?
- Would you get a different response from your mother, your father or another key figure in your childhood? How?
- Do you find it easy or difficult to trust? Why?
- How would your parents express their feelings for each other (and, if relevant, their new partners)?

- How did your relationship with your parents change when you became a teenager?
- Have you ever felt rejected by either of your parents? Why?
- Did you feel that one of your parents would try to get you on their side?
- Did you feel in competition with your brother, sister, step- or half-siblings?
- What might other people consider to be different about your family?

2. Put your answers to one side and come back after an hour or so and highlight everything that strikes you as important. Do any keywords or phrases appear? What are the themes?

3. Next think about your most important adult relationships; how have you dealt with these themes yourself?

4. What have been the most contentious issues in your past adult relationships? How did your parents cope with these issues?

5. How has your childhood affected your self-esteem?

Summing Up

Our view of ourselves is inextricably linked with the view in the mirror held up by our parents, caregivers and siblings. If they offered qualified or conditional love, we can have trouble truly accepting and loving ourselves. Understanding this legacy is the first step towards making peace with ourselves and improving our self-esteem.

IN A NUTSHELL:

- Make a commitment to understand your childhood and how it formed the person you are today.
- Take off both the rosy glasses that allow you to see only the good in the past and the dark glasses that record only the bad.
- Your goal is to be able to look yourself in the eye and say: 'I'm OK.'

STEP 2

LET GO OF
THE PAST

In the workshops I run on improving self-esteem, I sometimes meet resistance to the idea that our childhood shapes our picture of ourselves today. It's not that people disbelieve me, but something makes them uncomfortable.

'I hate the way that therapists always blame everything on the past,' said Imogen, thirty-two. She wanted to press on to some of the practical confidence-building exercises later in the programme but reluctantly agreed to look back: 'I had a really great childhood. My father had this knack of turning everything into an adventure. I remember once setting off to the seaside really early, suitcases on the roof-rack; I'd really been looking forward to this holiday because we didn't go away very often. However, for some reason we never really got there. I'm a bit hazy on this because I was only young, but we turned round and headed back home again. I remember the song he made up – "Daddy drives the car along" to the tune of "Michael, row the boat ashore" – but not why we abandoned the holiday.'

Can you guess now? I asked.

'My mother had serious mental health problems and I think she must have been overwhelmed or something, but my father covered up for her.' Having an erratic parent must have been frightening for a small child, but one of the ways that Imogen coped was by shutting out large chunks of her childhood and focusing on the good bits. But before she could move forward, Imogen needed to address her past.

If you're struggling to accept the importance of your childhood, maybe you don't want to focus on bad memories or be disloyal to your parents; the second step to loving yourself works hand in hand with the first and should help overcome resistance.

The Power of Forgiveness

There is an important idea at the centre of this chapter which will not only free you from the past but also transform your opinion of yourself. It is also the foundation for the work in the rest of the book. So what is this idea? In a word: forgiveness.

Unfortunately, there are two myths about forgiveness which stop people from moving on. The first is that forgiveness is a feeling. For many years, I fell into this trap myself and thought of forgiveness as something inside your stomach. Do I forgive someone? The answer was a gut feeling. However, the more I've thought and the more I've worked with people, I've discovered that forgiveness is as much an intellectual decision as a feeling. You can decide to forgive someone and this choice will trigger the emotional change inside. (More about this later.)

The second myth about forgiveness is that it is something for the person who has wronged you. It goes along with the idea that forgiveness has somehow to be earned. However, forgiveness is a gift to yourself. I know this sounds weird but let me explain. For many years, I hated a boy who bullied me when I arrived at my primary school. I can still remember the cruel look on his face and the nasty taunts. However, hating this boy kept him in my life, so while I've forgotten the names and faces of most of my classmates, even my friends at the time, he was preserved in my life – like an insect in amber. I sort of knew this was stupid, but I didn't realise how stupid until I watched a television talk show where guests were given the chance to confront their old nemeses.

Most of these guests were in tears remembering the cruelty and how the opinions of these people (from ten or even fifteen years ago) had blighted their lives. Time after time, the bully would come on and have no recollection of their victims. They were complete strangers. By continuing to hold a grievance, the bullied had not been punishing the perpetrators or holding them to account; they were punishing themselves. This is why forgiveness is a gift to yourself. It is not about forgetting what happened but about not allowing it to spoil your life today.

So how do you go about forgiving your parents, siblings and schoolmates who have undermined your self-belief? First of all you need to identify and examine your grievances. For Imogen, whom we met earlier, this was a breakthrough:

'I never realised how angry I felt with my mother for abandoning me and my sister when she went into hospital. Dad did everything to fill the gap but there was this huge hole in our lives and I don't even know how long she was away for but, at the time, it felt like for ever.'

'Have you forgiven her?' I asked.

Imogen shook her head. 'I can't until I accept that she did hurt me – however unwittingly.'

UNHOOKING THE PAST

Whether your parents were great or not so great, one of the key tests of being a true adult is having a rounded view of them: acknowledging both their strengths and weaknesses; accepting their mistakes as well as celebrating their achievements.

1. Detach yourself for a moment:
    • Don't be tempted to blame your parents. They are just as much the products of their upbringing as you are of yours.
    • Conversely, don't defend their actions either, as too much time justifying their behaviour can stop you from seeing the patterns.

2. Make connections:
    • Find three examples of how you are like your mother.
    • Find three examples of how you are like your father.
    • If you did not know one or both of your parents, find another significant carer whose personality has had an impact on you.

3. What do you like/dislike?
    • Make a list of all the positive and negative legacies from your parents.

- Are there any links between the two? A positive – for example, seeing both sides of the argument – is often the flip side of a negative, for example: unemotional.

4. When are you most likely to behave like one of your parents?
   - Think of an example at work.
   - Think of an example with friends.
   - Think of an example with a boyfriend/girlfriend/partner.

5. What are the alternative ways of behaving?
   - Brainstorm as many as possible.
   - What is missing from your list?
   - Maybe ask a friend to come up with other alternatives.
   - The last idea or the most outlandish can sometimes be the key.

An example: Paulo came from a family that rarely argued and found himself attracted to confident, outgoing women. However, they would often get extremely angry. He had always tried to appease (like his father did) but this rarely worked or left him dissatisfied. When we brainstormed the alternatives, he kept finding variations on the same theme: walk away, don't go home, rationalise the argument. Finally, I asked: 'What about getting angry too, or fighting your corner?' It hadn't even crossed his mind as a possibility. Ultimately, this was the breakthrough in his counselling.

Developing Compassion

So far in the journey towards forgiveness, we have acknowledged and understood our own hurts and regrets. The next ingredient is to develop some compassion for our parents.

Carrie, in her mid-forties, had a painful childhood. 'I absolutely adored my father but my mother made my life a misery. Dad would take me to work events and outings, while my mother stayed at home. He was interested in my school work and forever praised me and made me feel special. I hated to be left alone with my mum because she used to be really spiteful – pulling my hair and slapping me for the slightest misdemeanour. Sometimes when Dad went to his sister's – whom my mother hated – he would leave me behind at home. I used to particularly dread those occasions because Mum would really take it out on me.'

As you can imagine, Carrie's opinions, as a child, were pretty black and white: mother = bad, and father = good. However, as an adult, she found a more balanced view: 'In many ways, I'm angry with my father for not protecting me. He must have guessed what used to happen. Even when he was around he could be weak and did not like to stand up to my mother. With hindsight, it was strange to take me to adult parties – even back then it must have raised eyebrows – and what must it have been like for my mother?

Later, after my father died, Mum and I became much closer and she told me about the man she loved but who died during the war. Really she should never have married Dad – but they were Catholic and divorce was a mortal sin. I guess she was an unhappy woman. Today she would have asked for help but these things were not talked about in her generation.' Ultimately, Carrie had developed compassion for her mother. So how do you go about this?

1. Imagine that you are a lawyer and putting together a case for the defence.

   • **Look for mitigating circumstances.** Are you judging your parent through today's eyes and not taking into consideration the prevailing beliefs of the time? What resources would your parent have needed to act differently?

- **Why do you think your mother or father behaved as they did?** What sort of childhood did they have? What problems were they up against?

- **What witnesses – like your siblings or your aunts and uncles – could provide a positive character reference?** You can either imagine interviewing them in your head, or, even better, discuss your feelings about your childhood with them. Even without prompting, they will naturally put forward a defence for your mother or father.

- **List all your mother's or father's good qualities.** It is human nature to take for granted the good things of life and become obsessed by what we lack. So think about the positives from your childhood which someone less fortunate might have longed for. In Carrie's case, she remembered her mother's clean and ordered house, and how she always made sure that her daughter was well turned out.

2. Imagine that you are a prosecution lawyer looking over the case of your favoured parent.

- **What was your mother's or father's greatest weakness?** If you find this question hard, try turning it round and identifying his or her greatest strength – as normally our bad qualities are the flip side of our good ones. For example, Carrie's father's greatest strength was that he loved his daughter so strongly. Conversely, his greatest weakness was that this left him little energy to love his wife.

- **With your favoured parent, how much is your opinion based on how you would like to see them and how much on solid evidence?** Particularly if one parent was always away through their work or you saw less of them after divorce, it is easy to fantasise and turn them into the perfect parent rather than admit your disappointments.

- **Who would provide a balancing viewpoint?** How did your favoured parent behave towards your brother or sister? If you were their favourite, what impact did it have on everybody else in the family? What was the downside to being your mother or father's favourite? Did you find it hard to break away and do your own thing? Did you feel under a lot of pressure to achieve?

3. How did your behaviour contribute to the problems?

- **Look at all your beliefs about your parents.** Write all these beliefs down on the left-hand side of a piece of paper and then find an example to illustrate each one and write that down on the right-hand side. Carrie wrote for beliefs: 'My mother was not interested in me.' And for an example: 'She never came to my parent open evenings.' Cover over your list of beliefs on the left side and look at just the examples on the right. What would someone think who is unaware of the hidden belief? Could they guess the hidden belief from the example? Is there a different conclusion that could be drawn from your mother's or father's behaviour? Carrie, for example, admitted that her mother was shy and would be intimidated easily by the teachers.

- **Did you take sides?** It is hard not to be drawn into arguments, and being perceived as on the 'enemy' side will have coloured your less favoured parent's behaviour towards you.

- **Would you like to be closer to your mother or father but fear that it would be letting your other parent down?** Even though a divorce happened many years ago, it is easy to stay trapped in old patterns. Isn't it time to do what is best for you?

4. Are there any sticking points stopping a better relationship with one or both of your parents?

- **Write down all the unpleasant or hurtful things that your parent/s did.** It does not matter how trivial they might seem, put down everything that has caused pain. Start with your childhood and work up to the present day. Keep going until you can think of nothing more. Just putting everything down is cathartic.
- **Cross out anything that no longer bothers you.** This will show what you have already begun to forgive.
- **What is left?** Sometimes trivial things can hurt as much as major ones. If it still causes pain, it should be taken seriously and you should consider discussing it with your parents.

5. What if forgiveness was within your control?

- **Holding on to grudges keeps you stuck in the past.** By contrast, forgiveness will provide the key to a new relationship.
- **Resentment has a high price tag.** Research has shown that it contributes to higher blood pressure, stomach upsets and depression.
- **Not forgiving gives someone power over you.** It places you in the role of victim; a more powerful place to be is survivor.

6. What would happen if you discussed what still makes you angry with your father or mother? Although the idea will seem frightening at first, it is important to confront that fear as it is trapping you in the past. The following steps will increase the likelihood of a positive outcome.

- **Start with a positive.** It could be some of the things that you appreciate about him or her, maybe something that you have learned from reading this chapter or just your desire to have a better relationship.
- **Is there anything for which you would like to apologise?** This could encourage a reciprocal apology.

- **Explain what is stopping you from having a better relationship.** It helps if you are as specific as possible. To prevent misunderstanding and reduce the chance of the discussion escalating into an argument, try this formula: I feel . . . when you . . . because . . .

- **Sometimes just explaining your grievances is enough.** If you receive a full apology, that's brilliant. If your mother or father offers only justifications, make certain you listen with an open heart. You will generally learn more about her or him and this deeper understanding might make it easier for you to let go of past hurts.

7. How could you have a better relationship with your parents in the future?

- **Ultimately the most important relationship is the one that you have now.** Expecting a better relationship is halfway to experiencing one. You will certainly be more likely to interpret future behaviour through a positive lens rather than through the old, possibly distorted one.

- **What if you don't know how to contact your father or mother, they have addiction**

problems or are deceased? Try writing an imaginary letter or talking to their gravestone. This can release many pent-up feelings.

LETTING GO OF ANGER

There are two types of anger: Healthy Anger (when you recognise a problem and respond in a manner proportional to the offence) and Negative Anger (when you either repress your feelings and let them eat your insides or when you explode and react out of all proportion to the offence). Whichever your anger style, this exercise will help change your relationship with anger by slowing down your automatic reactions:

Step away: Instead of reacting straight away, take the dog for a walk, put on some music, have a cup of tea and a piece of cake or do some exercise.

Go to a beautiful place: If it is not possible to step away, go to a beautiful place in your mind. This could be a favourite beauty spot or a concert or the ballet. What can you see? What can you smell? What can you hear?

De-stress: Take deep breaths and clench and unclench your fists.

Deal with the problem: This could be half an hour later or the next day, but talk to the other person. If you are calm, they are more likely to listen and respond in a similar manner.

There is more about using anger in an appropriate manner in another book in this series: *Resolve Your Differences*.

A New Start – With Your Father

If you are a woman, improving your relationship with your father is key to improving your relationships with all men. For this reason, much of this exercise is aimed at women. If you are a man, a better relationship with your father will improve your confidence.

1. Assess your relationship with your father

- Do you tell your father as much about your personal life and private thoughts as you do your mother?
- Do you imagine that your father is less interested in these types of information or maybe that it is easier to stick to 'safe' topics?

- Do you often go through your mother to communicate with your father? (This is common
with daughter-and-father relationships).
- Have you put more time and energy into
getting to know your mother than into getting
to know your father?

If the answer is yes to any of these, you probably
treat your father differently from your mother and
in some way the relationship will have suffered.

2. Think of three occasions which sum up your relationship with your father

- These could be stories from your childhood
or just snapshots frozen in time. Put as much
detail as possible into these occasions. How
old are you? Where are you? What can you
see? What can you smell?
- What do these pictures tell you about your
relationship with your father?
- What does it say about his personality?

3. Reassess your defining moments

- Although these memories will have defined
your relationship with your father – in both the

past and the present – you need to remember that it is just *your* interpretation of events.

- So find a time *alone* with your father (this is important so that there is nobody to interrupt with their memories or to tell him 'he's got it all wrong') and ask what he remembers. Be careful not to be judgmental or to accuse him. Just ask: 'Do you remember . . .?' For example, Charlotte – the woman with high self-esteem from Chapter One – asked: 'Do you remember Monday mornings when you set off for a week of work away from home?' She had always hated the fact that he did not turn back and see her waving. She thought he valued his job more highly than her and could not wait to be off. The truth was very different. 'I hated Monday mornings,' he told her. 'I would focus on putting my key in the car lock rather than see the look on your and your mother's face. That would have made it even harder. Some mornings my hands would shake with holding back the tears.'

- Be ready to ask supplementary questions. How did you feel? What else was going on in your life at that point?

- Even if he remembers things differently, do not interrupt but keep nodding your head and making encouraging noises, like 'I see' and 'Yes'.

- How do your father's memories change your impression of him?

4. Assess how your father changed

- Your defining memories – the glasses through which you will interpret his behaviour – will have happened during your childhood.
- These are normally the years when men are most caught up in their careers – partly because men are more ambitious in their twenties and thirties than when they are older, and partly because they will have felt driven to succeed and provide the best for their children.
- After the age of about forty-five, many men have the weight of 'being a success' taken off their shoulders and can breathe more easily. Meanwhile, you will have started to work and gain insight into the pressures on your father.
- So both you and your father are different people, but all too often your relationship today is still being filtered and distorted by the past.

5. Make a commitment to a better relationship

- Try to communicate with open ears, an open mind and an open heart.
- Make more of an effort – invest as much time and energy in the relationship with your father as you already do with your mother (this is especially important for women where there can often be a large disparity between daughter/mother time and daughter/father time).
- Spend time with your father alone. (You probably already do this with your mother.)
- Draw your father out. Ask him about his relationship with his own father. What are his greatest achievements? What are his regrets? How has being a father changed him?
- Intimate conversations normally happen when you are doing something else. So ask him to share a skill with you – for example: wallpapering or gardening.

6. Understand your different ways of communicating

- There are two ways of approaching a problem. The first is to talk through all the feelings and wait for a solution to emerge. The second is to take the feelings as given and try to fix the problem. The first places great emphasis on emotions and the second on rationality. In general, women tend to use the first approach and men the second.

- Both strategies are equally valid but daughter-and-father communication is often hampered because a daughter with a problem expects an emotional response but gets a rational one.

- When we share a problem or a piece of news, we are usually looking for one or more of the following: approval, sympathy and advice.

- When Amy, thirty, decided to go freelance, as the first step to setting up her own business, she was worried about her father's reaction. Indeed, after talking to her father she felt judged: 'He asked lots of questions, like he thought I was making the biggest mistake in my life. It seems he has no confidence in my decisions or ability; I felt totally belittled.' In contrast, her mother was great: 'She was really excited and gave me her full support.' Actually, Amy came away with the wrong impression. Both her parents were trying to nurture her but her father thought she wanted advice, her mother guessed – rightly in this case – that she wanted approval.

7. Improve your communication

- Rather than expecting your father to guess what response you need, for example, sympathy or advice, be up-front and tell him.
- When Amy used this strategy, she told her dad: 'I really value your opinions on my business, and your experiences, but I need to know that you approve first.' She was surprised to discover that her father was really proud of her. He had wanted to do something similar himself but had had a young family and judged the idea too risky. Later, Amy asked her father's advice and he discovered a hole in her business plan.
- Remember your father's questioning and rationalising is partly to help him understand your choices. He will naturally worry – as he wants the best for you – and this is his way of reassuring himself that you will be OK.

8. If you're still feeling judged

- Look at your father's motives, not his style.
- Ask yourself who is doing the judging. Sometimes we are so quick to judge ourselves that even the smallest question from our fathers – 'Have you thought about . . . ?' – can

be heard as damning. Are you, in effect, criticising your father for something that you are actually doing to yourself?

- Tell him the effect that his communication style is having on you. For example: 'I get the impression that you think I'm making a big mistake' or 'I feel you're angry with me . . .' This will give him the opportunity either to change direction or to correct your reading of his response.

- Value the rational way. Some men offer their daughters and sons unquestioning and all-embracing support. Although this feels wonderful, it is very similar to how we treat small children. Maybe your father is giving you the compliment of treating you like a grown-up?

A New Start – With Your Mother

In an ideal world, we would have a close relationship with both of our parents. Unfortunately, a lot of my clients find their father a rather distant figure and although they feel closer to their mother, sometimes it feels too close. (If you wonder what I mean by 'too close', see parts one and two of this section.) I have paired 'A New Start – With Your Mother' and 'A New Start – With Your Father'. This is because our relationship with our father is directly influenced by our relationship with our mother and vice versa.

1. 'I love my mother but . . .'

Women get a lot of their identity and self-respect out of being a good mother. So even the slightest criticism of mothers can make us either agitated or angry. Maybe you felt something similar about the suggestion that you might be too close to yours? Be patient with me and answer the following questions:

- When you were a child, did you feel that your mother sacrificed more than your father?
- Do you, in some way, see your father through your mother's eyes?
- Did you become your mother's confidant/ confidante or adviser over problems with your father?
- Did your mother ever poke fun at your father over small failings, over-supervise, criticise or not allow him an equal voice on parenting?
- Do you feel responsible for your mother's happiness?

- How would your mother feel if you told your father something personal before you told her?
- Do you discuss your personal problems – with the exception of financial matters – with your mother first?
- How would she feel if you phoned and just spoke to your father?
- What would your mother's reaction be if you and your father spent a weekend alone together? Would she be jealous or maybe just uncomfortable – even though she might have spent lots of time alone with you herself? (This question is especially relevant for daughters.)
- Do you ever feel that you are siding with your mother because your father did not or does not treat her fairly?
- Is your mother number one in your eyes?

2. Reassess your relationship with your mother

- If you answered yes to any of the questions above, you need to reassess your relationship with your mother – even if you felt that she made more sacrifices than your father.

Unfortunately, men's work – like arranging mortgages and insurance policies or fixing things – is less visible to children. Many men continue with jobs they hate in order to support their families or endure long commutes so their families can live in bigger houses or enjoy a better lifestyle.

- Do you feel guilty about answering 'yes' to any of the questions? If so, be reassured that most people agree with at least one of these statements.

- As your mother was probably responsible for the majority of your care as a baby, the bond will be close. However, it should not be so close that your father has felt excluded and therefore less involved in your life.

- In some cases, the relationship between mother and child can become so close that her emotional needs are met by her son or daughter rather than by her husband. This is what I mean by 'too close'.

- Parenting is not a competitive sport. Sadly, some mothers feel the need to be 'number one' in their children's lives.

3. Give your mother and father equal parenting rights

- Especially as an adult, you should feel able to have a good relationship with your father without feeling, in some way, that you are 'letting your mother down'.
- If you spend time with just your mother, you should do the same with your father.

4. What if my father does not deserve it?

- Imagine that you are a detective, new to this case, and interview your father; assume nothing and listen, without prejudice, to his side.
- Have your mother's opinions been turned into beliefs and, over time, become your hardened facts?
- What is the proof? Would it stand up in a court of law where the defendant has the benefit of the doubt?
- In twenty-five years' experience of counselling couples, I have yet to find a regular couple who are not equally responsible for their problems.

- Even in cases with addiction and violence, the concept of innocent and guilty is still murky. How much did your mother 'enable' or 'excuse' your father's bad behaviour?
- Ultimately, nobody knows what goes on in the privacy of other people's marriages. It is both pointless and counterproductive to take sides.

5. Mothers are wonderful but they are not beyond criticism

- When issues are not addressed, they fester and turn a basically good relationship sour.
- Often everybody is aware of forbidden subjects but ignores them.
- This is particularly common in the mother–child relationship where everybody wants to keep things 'nice'.
- If you were 100 per cent honest, what would you say to your mother?
- What do you think her reaction would be? What are your fears?

6. Decide what personality traits you share with your mother

- If you become touchy around your mother, or her behaviour sets you on edge, write down everything that really gets to you.

- Go down the list and ask yourself: Have I ever done something similar?

- Much as we vow at sixteen to be nothing like our parents, we almost inevitably turn into them – the process seems to speed up as we head towards or pass forty.

- Often the things that make us most angry about our mother is the part of her that we recognise in ourselves.

7. Ask her: How can I make your life better?

- If you feel responsible for your mother's happiness – perhaps she is alone and elderly or suffers from depression – this is particularly important.

- Our general sense of anxiety can send us off in dozens of different directions and waste our energies in something that might be appreciated but is, ultimately, unnecessary.

- A lot of people worry about asking: How can I make your life better? They fear that the floodgates might open. My experience is that most mothers ask for something small – like regular phone calls.

8. Remember: your mother is an adult and responsible for her own life

- Do you ever treat your mother like a small child?
- She might find this irritating but does not say anything for fear of upsetting you.
- Does your 'closeness' stop her developing friendships and her own coping skills?
- Does your 'closeness' stop you from developing relationships?

FORGIVING YOURSELF

This is another important ingredient for letting go of past anger, resentment and pain. It is amazing how many negative feelings we can hold against ourselves. Thinking of something from the past about which you have regrets, answer the following questions:

- What knowledge would you have needed to have acted differently?

- What skills would you have needed?
- What handicaps did you face?
- What are the mitigating circumstances?
- Who is being hurt the most by your anger, resentment and pain?
- How would your life be different if you could just forgive yourself?

The Final Ingredient for Forgiveness

Having identified past hurts, examined them and developed compassion for the people who, often unwittingly, inflicted pain on you, you are almost ready to decide to forgive. There is one final task: identifying the lessons.

At first sight, there is nothing to be gained from negative experiences. Surely they are best forgotten? However, in most circumstances, something positive can be salvaged. Imogen, whom we met earlier, looked at me blankly when I suggested that she ask herself: 'What could possibly be the lesson I learned from my mother, beyond don't get sick?' However, when she thought further, she discovered that there was something. 'I suppose that I've been more aware of other people's problems and less quick to judge.'

For Carrie, whose Dad took her to work events but left her mother at home, her gift was to face up to her problems: 'I hoped my marriage problems would somehow go away if I kept busy and did not think too much about them – just like my mother did. However, hoping never changed anything for her.' Fortunately, Carrie took the lesson from her mother's relationship and made changes in her own.

Finally, my childhood bully taught me to look at my own behaviour and to consider whether my reactions might have encouraged him. All these years later, he's also given me a story for this book. Much as I'd rather not have had these gifts, I will accept them with thanks.

Summing Up

Although we need to understand the impact of our childhood on our life today, it is pointless to blame our parents. They are the products of their own childhood. It is therefore important to forgive our parents' shortcomings as much as to thank them for their strengths. Forgiveness is as much an intellectual decision as an emotional response. So identify and examine past grievances, develop compassion for both the people who hurt you and for yourself and, finally, acknowledge the lessons – however unwanted.

IN A NUTSHELL:

- Forgiveness is an act of generosity to someone else but a gift to yourself.
- Forgiving other people makes it easier to forgive yourself.
- Start small when changing your relationship with your parents. Think about one thing you could do differently.

STEP

3

DON'T LET OTHER PEOPLE RUN YOU DOWN

When you were a child, did your mother or father say: 'Sticks and stones may break my bones but words will never hurt me?' There is a lot of wisdom in this old saying, but although other people's opinions leave no visible wounds on the outside, they can cause deep invisible scars inside. For someone with a low opinion of himself or herself, any adverse comment is doubly painful because it reinforces a negative self-image. If this sounds familiar, next time you hear something critical, stop and ask yourself three questions:

• Why am I bothered what other people think?
• Do they really think that badly of me?
• Am I leaping to conclusions about what others think?

This chapter will help you answer these questions.

Understand and Deal With Projection

Have you ever watched someone giving a presentation at work overreact to even the mildest question and take it as an outright attack? Does your partner sometimes hear a completely different meaning from the one that you intended? Have you been on a date when someone has accused you of bad intentions without knowing enough about you to form a proper judgement? All these are examples of a common phenomenon called *projection*. To explain more, let me tell you a story from my childhood.

My grandfather had a cine-camera and he would film important family events – such as the christenings of my sister and myself. Years later, on Sunday evenings, we would beg our father to show the films over and over again. The silent flickering images would be projected on to the living-room wall or on to a portable screen, if my father could be bothered to set it up. I found these family images and the clues to everybody's relationship completely fascinating, probably an early indication of my future career. If my sister or I needed to go to the lavatory or the kitchen, the only way out of the living room was past the screen, and, for a few seconds, the faces of grand-parents, aunts, uncles and cousins would be projected on to our faces.

I tell this story because it illustrates one aspect of projection. When someone responds in an over-the-top way to us – either positively or negatively – it probably says more about them than us. We have unwittingly become the blank screen on to which they have projected their opinion of someone else or some feeling that belongs to them. Often the less someone knows about us – the blanker we are to them – the more likely they are to be able to project their needs, emotions or expectations on to us.

A common example would be someone who had a difficult relationship with their father, projecting that role (almost his face, too) on to their boss. Although repeatedly rebelling against a superior, or having an overwhelming need for approval, might seem a work problem, it is often acting out old family dynamics – with colleagues standing in for brothers and sisters. This same process happens a lot with celebrities and public figures. Princess Diana became such a potent icon because we seldom heard her, we just saw photographs or film of her arriving at a premiere or a hospice. We could project our needs on to her, too. This is why people who actually knew Diana found her so at odds with her public image – which had been projected on to her and therefore said more about us than about her.

The psychological term 'projection' was invented by Freud, who used it in a very specific way. He discovered that his patients would first deny unpleasant feelings – or something that contradicted their image of themselves – and then further distance themselves by projecting the negatives on to someone else. The classic example would be a man who had hidden homosexual tendencies. Particularly before gay liberation, this man could have had a secret hatred of himself. Of course, he would deny those feelings but he could go one step further and project his hatred on to gay men in general and might even go so far as to beat one up. The colloquial term for this kind of projection is dumping. For example, we might be angry with someone at work who never stops talking – not just because it is irritating, but because our colleague's behaviour reminds us of our own failure to listen.

However, it is not just negative things that belong to us that we project on to others; it can be positive things too. For example, Chloe, twenty-three, wanted to be an actress. When she started classes in the evening she put great store on the experience of her teacher: 'He's been in several well-known television shows – although in small parts – and toured throughout the country and has great connections in the industry.' She saw him as the fountain of all knowledge – which made her a very attentive pupil. However, when it came to casting the end-of-term play, Chloe got little more than a walk-on part and she was completely devastated. 'He obviously doesn't think I'm up to it. I'll never make a go of acting,' she complained in one of my workshops. So I helped her take back her projection that her teacher had all the answers. What about future directors and casting agents, would they all have the same opinion? 'I don't know,' she admitted, 'acting is very subjective and it's all down to personal taste.' What about the lead role? 'I'm too young for it and I suppose there are other people who are better suited,' she explained. Chloe had begun to take back her projection and make her own value judgements.

The important thing to stress is that *everybody* is projecting all the time – both favourable and unfavourable characteristics, behaviours and attitudes. So we need to be aware not only of our own projections, but also of what other people might be projecting on to us.

When we are looking for love, this natural tendency to project goes into overdrive. On the first few dates, a new man or woman is a blank screen on to whom we can play out our dreams, our fears and the bits of ourselves that we don't really like. Sometimes projection can help make a strong initial connection and sometimes it can hold us back.

Take Claude, who is a thirty-four-year-old gay man, who agreed to be interviewed for this book. We had met in a bar and although it was quiet, he attracted appreciative glances. So I wondered why Claude was single. 'My father was very domineering, he did not like music or people coming round to the house,' he explained. 'I'm thirteen years younger than my brothers and sister – who left home early – and I was an unplanned mistake who stopped his freedom.' It soon emerged that Claude did not consider himself attractive. So where could his poor self-image have come from? 'Dad called me "Cockroach" – it was supposed to be affectionate, but I'm sure that you get the picture. As a young man, my father had been very handsome. You should see the pictures. But as an older man, he looked exactly like I do now. It's quite uncanny. Although I didn't go through the gorgeous stage.' It is clear that

Claude's father had projected his ambivalence about his loss of looks on to his son and made him into the ugly one.

'What do you think if someone is attracted to you?' I asked him, aware of the hungry eyes of some of the other clientele in the bar. 'If someone likes me, it's strange,' he replied. 'I probably think that they have poor taste.'

'That there is something wrong with them?' I confirmed.

He nodded sadly. Not only was Claude struggling with the projection from his father but he, in turn, was also projecting his own sense of being damaged goods on to his dates. It is not surprising that Claude has had just two relationships – the longest of which had lasted only six months.

Another example of projection is Samantha, thirty-three, who came to see me after a series of unsuccessful relationships. 'Men are so false, they pretend to be great and I'm suckered into thinking this one might be different, but you know what? They all let you down.' Samantha had no trouble forming relationships – in fact, she quickly became involved – but none of her relationships seemed to last. She thought the problem was her dates, and wanted me to offer advice on how to change them, but I suspected that she was projecting something on to these men.

Samantha explained that the relationships started very well. 'We have lots in common, we like similar things and we laugh a lot. But actually they're putting on a show and, slowly but surely, I discover that actually they are quite selfish or spend too much time at their mother's – you get the picture?' It soon emerged that Samantha was desperate to be in a relationship and have a family. She tried not to let her fantasies get in the way and to remain level-headed, but actually she was projecting an ideal man on to these dates. No wonder she liked them so much at the beginning. But her new boyfriend could not remain a blank sheet – over a few dates she would start to get to know the real person – and Samantha would end up feeling deceived. In many ways projecting positive qualities can be just as problematic as projecting bad ones.

With projection influencing how we behave towards other people, it is important not only that we understand how it works but also that we learn how to deal with the results. In my experience, whether handled well or badly, projection moves through five phases: recognition, exaggeration, distortion, confusion and resolution.

The Five Phases of Projection

Using Samantha as an example, this is what happens as we progress from a first meeting through to knowing someone well:

1. Recognition

Something about a stranger encourages us to project our desires, our expectations or something about ourselves on to them. While I was counselling Samantha, she was dating a new man. Her eyes were shining as she talked about him. He was a businessman and although he was younger, he 'believed in commitment'. I have put the last part of her description in quotation marks because, at this early stage of counselling, I had no means to know whether this claim was true or not. I had only Samantha's version of their first few dates. However, the glowing reports were probably a projection: she had wanted him to behave in a certain way and had interpreted his behaviour to fit those expectations. Yet it is more complex than the boyfriend being just a blank screen. The projection needs to stick – rather than slide off. Think of it as a hook provided by the boyfriend. Although I was sceptical about the long-term potential for this relationship – considering Samantha's track record – some part of this man was fed up with the single lifestyle too and on some level, either consciously or unconsciously, he had provided a hook for the projection.

2. Exaggeration

Next, you notice and exaggerate the behaviour that fits in with your beliefs. Through Samantha's eyes, her boyfriend staying over on Saturday night and not leaving until after supper on Sunday showed not only that he was keen but also that the relationship was getting 'serious'. Alternatively, he could have had nothing better to do or, being a single man, he might have appreciated a hot, home-cooked meal – but Samantha could not even consider this option. Every positive scrap of evidence was being exaggerated.

3. Distortion

The longer two people spend together, the better they get to know each other. There are also more dates or social/business encounters to provide information about character and intentions. During this phase, events that do not fit are downplayed or ignored. When first describing her boyfriend, Samantha had mentioned his ex-girlfriend and a small child in passing but because they 'lived the other side of the country' they 'were not an issue'. This is clearly a distortion of the truth.

4. Confusion

There comes a point where it becomes harder to reconcile what we would like to believe and the evidence. The result is confusion and we feel uncomfortable that the other person does not behave in line with our projections and expectations. Samantha was upset because her boyfriend had disappeared off to the West Country for the weekend to visit his son. Her tears seemed to say: 'If he is so committed to this relationship, how can he abandon me?'

Other information began to emerge about her boyfriend. Previously she had described him as a businessman but now he had been downgraded to a self-employed builder. Later in our session, Samantha complained that she was being given 'mixed messages'. On the one hand, he had disappeared for the weekend, but on the other, he had been jealous of her going out with friends. 'It was like he cared what I got up to, but actually he had no right to tell me what to do,' she said. Samantha was truly in the confused phase.

5. Resolution

Ultimately the differences between projection and reality can no longer be resolved. In Samantha's case the relationship ended after six weeks. She decided that he had been leading her on and did not want a relationship after all. But how much had been her projection and how much his behaviour?

UNHOOKING YOUR PROJECTIONS

When you meet someone new and have a strong reaction – either positive or negative – try out this exercise. It also works with casual acquaintances – perhaps a colleague at work – whom you dislike but cannot put your finger on exactly why.

1. Recognition

Take a long dispassionate look at this stranger. Does he or she remind you of anybody? Maybe their face, a quirk or the way they move? What about their behaviour? Next think about the behaviour or attitude that grates and then take a deep breath. Could the same criticism be levelled at you?

2. **Exaggeration**

   Once you are aware why this stranger provokes such a strong reaction, watch and double-check that you have found the right reason. Could there be anything else to add? In particular, look to see if you are 'dumping' on him or her.

3. **Distortion**

   This is the most important phase. Look for evidence that the stranger is not like your mother, father, brother, sister. When you feel persecuted, for example, by her loud voice or his demand that you repeat something at work, tell yourself: she is not my mother or he is not my brother.

4. **Confusion**

   Repeat the above part of the exercise on a couple of separate occasions, so you create a longer and longer list of contrary evidence. You will soon be surprised that you ever thought that stranger was like your family member or reminded you of yourself. In effect, you have stopped projecting.

5. **Resolution**

   Finally, look back at what you can learn about yourself. If you have been projecting your feelings about a family member, it is probably time to reassess your relationship with this person. Consider talking over old gripes or challenging their behaviour today. If it is something that you dislike about yourself that you have projected on to a stranger, how could you work on that facet of your behaviour?

Self-esteem and the Approval of Other People

When it comes to other people's opinions, we can sometimes take two contradictory approaches. If someone says something negative, we take it on board without question. However, when they offer a compliment, we downplay the praise or discount it altogether: 'Oh, this old thing' or 'It was nothing' or 'The main course was good but the dessert left something to be desired.' Not only does your partner, friend or boss feel rejected or hurt but also your self-esteem remains low. So next time someone says nothing nice, don't run yourself down. Just say 'Thank you' and enjoy the moment.

Next time someone reacts negatively – especially if it is out of all proportion – remember projection. They are probably trying to dump their feelings on to you. Imagine their bad mood as a box – picture it with a bow on top. Just because it has been offered doesn't mean that you have to take it. Keep your imaginary hands by your sides and let it drop harmlessly on to the floor.

Next time someone is critical – especially if they are trying to be helpful – try and accept it as a gift. Your automatic response might be: he's running me down or she doesn't like me. However, this person could be offering constructive feedback and some suggestions on how to perform better. Keep focused on what actually is being said, and don't add extra embellishments of your own, or you will miss what the other person did like.

SEEK OUT POSITIVE PEOPLE

Look through your address book and decide which of the following categories your friends fall into:

Negative: Life is terrible for these friends or work colleagues, nobody understands them and the world is going to the dogs. They are always whinging and although they might seem supportive they are really only interested in encouraging you to wallow in your problems. These people are particularly likely to run down their partners and encourage you to bond by complaining about yours too.

Uplifting: Life is a laugh, day-to-day activities are enjoyable and they're planning something fun for the future. These friends or work colleagues will find the positives and although they sometimes feel down, it is not for too long.

Destructive: Life is a competition and they have a more impressive car, job or their children are doing so much better than yours. These friends or work colleagues want to boost their self-esteem by making you feel dowdy in comparison. Worse still, some can even subtly run you down – or, in some cases, not so subtly.

Which category do the majority of your friends fall into? How could you spend more time with uplifting friends? How could you spend less time with negative friends as they can really pull you down? Why are you putting up with destructive friends?

Summing Up

It is difficult to base our self-esteem on what other people think. On many occasions, they hold up a distorting mirror. Equally, we can project our difficult feelings on to other people and have a distorted picture of them. Learning to recognise when someone is projecting and learning to recognise our own projections, leads to better and happy relationships with ourselves and the people we care about.

IN A NUTSHELL:

- Accept that not everybody will like you.
- When someone has a very negative reaction, remember that it says more about them than about you.
- Practise accepting praise.

STEP 4

REPROGRAMME
YOUR INNER VOICE

If you find it hard to love yourself enough, it will be not just other people bringing you down but a small voice inside your own head as well. Instead of supporting you – 'This is a setback that can be overcome' – it is more likely to berate: 'Idiot! Why did you do that?' In fact, our inner voice is crueller to ourselves than we'd ever permit anyone else to be. So in this step, I look at the kinds of things our inner voice is saying and how to reprogramme a message from a negative to a positive.

Limited Thinking

Have you ever envied people who throw themselves into new experiences and always appear supremely confident? Nothing seems to stop them, while there are countless obstacles preventing you from making even the first step. So what is the difference between these go-getters and everybody else? Successful people either don't see limits, or see a way round them; meanwhile unconfident people are handicapped by limited thinking. Here is an example of limited thinking in action at a party:

- I am not attractive or interesting.
- If I approach people I will be rejected.
- Therefore I will only respond if someone approaches me.
- Nobody I find attractive has approached me, which proves that I'm neither attractive nor interesting.

This kind of thinking not only keeps people trapped on the edges of life but also becomes a self-fulfilling prophecy. Worse still, one or two unfortunate experiences are built up and generalised into a global picture. Martina, twenty-eight, had two older and successful sisters who seemed to get everything they wanted. 'I'm not lucky, I don't get the breaks,' she explained in a workshop on loving yourself enough. I guessed that she was not only under-rating her abilities and intelligence but also not putting herself forward.

'What's stopping you volunteering to take on extra responsibilities or researching possible solutions to a problem at work?' I asked.

'I don't want other people to take advantage of me.' (Another example of limited thinking because one of her superiors might have admired and rewarded her initiative.)

'What makes you think that?'

'I did this work experience placement at a fashion magazine – really put my heart and soul into it. Of course, it didn't lead anywhere but then I'm not somebody's daughter or niece.'

As this must have happened at least ten years ago, I asked her for more recent examples, but Martina was struggling.

In most cases, limited thinking is built on a handful of central beliefs. Worse still, these beliefs are so familiar and taken for granted that we have not stopped and examined whether they are true or generalised from past experiences into totally different circumstances (for example, Martina worked in IT rather than fashion).

CHALLENGE YOUR CENTRAL BELIEFS

These fall into three different categories. Beliefs about ourselves: 'I can't stick at anything' or 'I always do my best'; beliefs about other people:

'Give an inch and people take a mile' or 'Smile and the world smiles with you'; and beliefs about the world: 'There's no such thing as a free lunch' or 'Hard work will be rewarded'.

- Write down as many beliefs as possible. What did your mother say? What about your father? What lessons did you get from school?

- Keep a notebook and during the next week capture as many beliefs as possible.

- Whenever you have a setback or a success, look at the experience and add more beliefs about yourself, other people and the world in general.

- When you have about fifty beliefs, go through them and total up the number of positive, enabling beliefs and the number which encourage limited thinking.

- With each of the negative beliefs, ask yourself: Where did it come from? What is the evidence? How is it damaging me? What's stopping me from discarding it?

- With the enabling beliefs, ask yourself: How can I build on this asset? What new things could I try?

Black-and-white Thinking

Another way that our inner voice can become toxic is by our seeing the world in very black-and-white terms. With this kind of thinking, something is either a complete success or a total failure. There is nothing in between. Sandy – an attractive forty-one-year-old with three children in their mid to late teens – felt exhausted and overwhelmed. She had been divorced for six years and had had a series of relationships that ranged from disappointing to disastrous. She sighed and said to me: 'You must think I am really screwed up.' Actually, I admired her honesty and readiness to look at the messy bits of her life. I could see that underneath the slightly aggressive exterior was a resourceful and loyal woman who would make someone a great partner.

Sandy had grown up in an all-female household. Her mother was a beautiful but rather vague woman who seemed to be forever in front of a mirror getting ready for her husband's return.

Sandy had a younger sister and a grandmother who lived with them. Her father, a businessman, was away during the week and, although he returned on Friday night, spent a lot of the weekend on the golf course. She described her father, who died a few years ago, as 'jealous, good-looking and lovely'. His work took him away for long stretches of time. In her father's absence, Sandy was in charge and would fix things around the house. It is not surprising that her expectation was that 'men are always going to leave'.

When listening to Sandy's story, I had been struck by how she saw herself in very black-and-white terms. At sixteen, she changed almost overnight from the 'nice schoolgirl' into an 'aggressive shoplifter'. In her marriage, 'the happy, devoted mum' who felt moulded by her husband (frequently away) became a 'good-time girl with a hangover who couldn't get out of bed in the morning'. Sandy's last two relationships seemed, on the surface, to be completely different. As she said: 'I have a different personality with every man.' The first man had been very laid-back and this brought out the opposite in Sandy. 'I'd got crazy jealous because he didn't seem to care and I became very insecure. So I'd do terrible things to get his attention, like sleeping with other men and hitting him.'

The second man was incredibly jealous and would go through her mobile phone checking her messages. 'I didn't really mind,' said Sandy. 'That was the sort of thing I used to do. So I understood.' Unfortunately, he would also get drunk at parties and accuse other men of paying her too much attention. On one occasion, he got into a fight with six bouncers outside a nightclub and the police were called. As Sandy explained: 'I became like one of those terrible women you see in television documentaries about binge drinking, screaming over and over: "Don't do it, don't do it".' He had promised to change and Sandy was thinking about letting him back into her house and her life. Why? 'With a jealous guy, I can be laid-back. No paranoid mornings or waking up drunk, I can be OK in the relationship,' she explained.

These might have been two different relationships but the dynamics were the same. In one relationship, Sandy played the 'jealous' role and in the other, the 'innocent' one.

When Sandy finished her story, I helped her look at how the pieces of the story fitted together. By understanding her relationship with her father, she began to make sense of her behaviour and stopped feeling, as she put it, like a 'freak'. She also began to question her own black-and-white thinking. Finally, she was ready to accept that she was not 'bad' but someone with a difficult child-hood who had made some poor choices – a much 'greyer' interpretation.

Sandy had also been using her relationships to prop up her poor self-image. Indeed, the former boyfriend begging for a second chance had done wonders. 'I don't think he realised how much he loved me until it was too late,' she said with a half-smile, probably entertaining private daydreams about saving him from his demons. However, rela-tionships are difficult enough without the added strain of propping up low self-esteem. What's more, there are other, and better, ways of feeling good about yourself. It was as though a light bulb had come on above Sandy's head. 'A new boyfriend might make me feel attractive, and good about myself, but it only works for a short while. If he doesn't phone, or we have an argument, my self-esteem drops through the floor. So really a new relationship is a rather high-risk strategy.'

In fact, there are millions of other ways of improving self-esteem. For example: walking the length of Hadrian's Wall, having a painting accepted for a local art exhibition, running a half-marathon, getting an Open University degree, or just simply shopping for an elderly neighbour. It is all a matter of taste and interest. Sandy had already gone back to work, expressly to improve her self-image, and had found a responsible and interesting position – an achievement for someone who had been out of the job market bringing up children. Instead of thinking only in black-and-white terms, Sandy had begun to register the greys in between.

GREMLINS ON MY SHOULDER

From time to time, I teach creative writing. I've been to schools, centres for the homeless, hospices and offices to help a wide range of people unlock their creativity and build up their confidence. The type of writing that my students find the most daunting is poetry (which is a shame because it is often the most fun, the quickest way to yield results and the most moving). Unfortunately, they believe that poetry is not written by someone like them, they didn't like poetry at school and they believe that, anyway, their work will be rubbish. This is a huge barrier to being creative, so I get everyone to close their eyes and imagine their negative thinking and negative voices are concentrated on a gremlin sitting on their shoulder, whispering nasty thoughts into their ears.

Next, we go round the room and everybody describes their gremlin and then flicks it off their shoulder. (Children have great fun drawing their gremlin and we pin them up on the walls.) Every time someone in the class says: 'My work's not very good' or 'I can't do this', I ask them to flick the gremlin off their shoulder. So try this for yourself:

- Close your eyes and picture your gremlin.

- What does it look like?

- What colour?

- How big?

- What are its nastiest features?

- What does its voice sound like?

- What does it say?

Next time your internal voice starts running you down, imagine that it is a gremlin on your shoulder and flick it off.

Pessimistic Thinking

When pessimists have a bad experience, they draw conclusions that are permanent ('I'm never going to find someone who is right for me'), all-pervasive ('The evening was ruined because I spilt coffee over everything') and personal ('I'm just not beautiful enough' or 'I don't earn enough'). By contrast, optimists, after a bad experience, will draw very different conclusions. The problems are particular ('The atmosphere in the restaurant was wrong'). They are temporary ('I was tired') or down to someone else ('he was not interested'). Most importantly, optimists view problems as surmountable: 'We didn't click on this occasion but I will meet the right guy' or 'Perhaps the second date will be better and she'll warm to me.'

There is a final twist to the difference between optimists and pessimists which is particularly cruel. While pessimists put bad things down to permanent causes and optimists to temporary ones, when it comes to good events, they swap over. So the pessimist thinks a success is just a fluke. Therefore, on a successful date, for example, the pessimist thinks: 'Wednesday was the club's cool night' or 'I put a lot of effort into researching everything' (temporary and specific reasons). Meanwhile, optimists expect the good times to last and think: 'I'm always lucky picking places to go to' or 'I know how to charm' (permanent and all-pervasive reasons). Is it any wonder, then, that pessimists find it hard to like – let alone love – themselves?

The following box underlines the differing attitudes to life.

Pessimist	Optimist
I'm ugly	I'm not looking my best today
Women don't like me	That woman didn't like me
Always	Sometimes
Never	Lately
I try hard	I'm talented
I'm not good at relationships	I've had some bad experiences
I can never remember birthdays	I was busy and forgot

Can I Change?

Despite all the handicaps in being a pessimist, I'm not suggesting pessimists become optimists and go around spouting uplifting statements such as: 'Today is the first day of the rest of my life.' There are benefits to mild pessimism, judiciously employed. In some professions – like lawyers who have to imagine the worst-case scenario – pessimism is a positive advantage. In addition, when things go wrong, pessimists are quick to put their hands up, take personal responsibility for their share of the failure and learn from the experience. By contrast, unbridled optimists just blame other people. In the worst cases, optimists can plunge from one disaster into another, forever hopeful, but learning nothing. Ultimately, the best place to be is somewhere between mild pessimism and qualified optimism.

Pessimism is just a way of looking at the world, albeit one so deeply ingrained that it has become a habit. The good news is that habits can be changed. Staying with the example about dating and low self-esteem, Gemma, who is thirty-eight, works in sales and slipped into depression after the failure of a six-month campaign to meet men. She had joined an Internet dating agency and had been set up by friends. One lunch date – in particular – had seemed hopeful. They had a lot in common – books and the theatre – but he had not phoned again. 'I don't know what I want from men,' she complained, 'and I don't know what is good for me.' She sat in my counselling room, defeated, and lapsed into silence. So I asked her about her lunch date: 'Everything I do around men is a failure.' What about the men off the Internet? She seemed to have been successful in setting up meetings. 'They're all after one thing,' she replied. I was at risk of becoming depressed too. How could I possibly help?

First, I needed to understand the myriad thoughts that had built these concrete conclusions. Gemma listed her problems: 'My age is against me – all the decent men can have their pick of much younger women.' 'Having children is a turn-off.' 'Nobody fancies me.' Her language was also very pessimistic: 'nobody', 'everything', 'all'. As a typical pessimist, she believed implicitly in her own conclusions. If someone else had said: 'Nobody fancies you', she would immediately have jumped to her own defence. However, because the messages came from a voice inside her head, they were accepted as gospel truth. When I simply repeated her statements back to her, she started to qualify them. 'OK, not everybody "doesn't fancy me", in fact, some of the men have come on strong,' she explained. 'Either I didn't like them or I felt that they were only offering casual sex.'

So a more accurate statement would have been: 'Some men don't fancy me.' A small shift but an important one. The next problem was that Gemma was mixing facts and opinions. How did she know that children were a turn-off? Had she done an extensive survey of all men? What about men who had a family and did not want more children? 'I suppose you're right,' she conceded, 'I don't have the pressure of the biological clock, although I do have to be back for the babysitter.' So I asked her to separate out the facts from the opinions. Fact: I have to get back home at a certain time and I'm less flexible about when I can meet up. Opinion: I feel that makes me less appealing than someone without responsibilities. Once again, it is a small change, but one that lets in a chink of hope.

The third problem for pessimists is always drawing the worst possible conclusions. Gemma was no exception. The friend of the friend had not phoned because she was 'too old'. While most things happen for a large number of reasons, pessimists always put it down to just one. So I went through a few alternatives with Gemma:

- He might have wanted a second date but was too busy at work; when things slackened he had felt the moment had passed.
- He might have had a phone call from an ex-flame and decided to try again.
- He might have liked her but only dated blondes.

Gemma smiled and accepted that all my reasons were possible too. When we discussed it further, Gemma admitted that her date had just finished a long-term relationship. Maybe he had been pressurised into the date by her friend and was simply not ready yet? If I had interviewed this man, I would have found a multitude of different and maybe competing reasons for his not calling. After all, we are complex creatures. So it is neither realistic nor helpful to put motives down to one damning reason – such as 'I'm too old'.

Finally, Gemma had built all her bad dating experiences into one catastrophic conclusion: 'Everything I do around men is a failure.' I remembered her job. Could she sell to men? How did she get on with her male colleagues? In fact, Gemma had no problems relating to men at work, it was just her personal life. Ultimately, Gemma discovered that she had let some bad experiences, plus her personal interpretations, build up into a hopeless picture. By challenging her pessimistic thought patterns, I had made the problems seem particular to her dates and therefore only temporary. In effect, Gemma had started to think like a guarded optimist.

STOPPING PESSIMISTIC THOUGHTS – EMERGENCY FIRST AID

When something bad happens, or you are under stress, it is easy to slip into an automatic pessimistic reaction. This exercise is aimed at stopping this destructive pattern.

Find something that will snap you out of your negative frame of mind. Some people have a rubber band round their wrist and ping it. Another idea is to keep a card with the word STOP written in large red letters in your wallet or bag. When you feel yourself falling into old patterns, bring it out and look at it. Finally, you could have a bell to ring. The choice is up to you – use anything that will bring you up short.

Next, remember the three golden rules:

1. It's not what happens but how I deal with it.

2. I can't control adversity but I can control my reactions to it.

3. I will look for the positives I can build on, rather than concentrating on the negatives I cannot.

Challenge Pessimistic Thoughts

The idea is to slow down automatic thinking and test the ideas in the real world:

1. **Recognise the thoughts.** This is hard as they are always second nature. So take a piece of paper and write down every opinion, interpretation or piece of information as it comes to you. Do not censor yourself; imagine you're taking dictation and write everything – no matter how stupid or unimportant it seems.
2. **Look at what you have written.** When I do this exercise with clients, the first surprise is that there is always less than they expected. Often our thoughts, trapped in our head, spiral out of control and become endless versions of the same thing. Writing everything down stops this from happening.
3. **Separate facts from opinions.** Facts can be proved. Facts stand up in court. Anything that involves interpretation or second-guessing is

opinion. For example, I made a fool of myself on the date. What is the evidence? Fact: I made a joke about ten useful things to do with a dead cat. Fact: She has a cat. Opinion: She thinks I'm insensitive and stupid. Another example: I had a real pig-out and blew my diet last night. What is the evidence? What is a pig-out? Fact: I ate a large packet of crisps last night. Opinion: I am a glutton.

4. **What are the consequences?** This is to help you understand how your pessimistic interpretations of events translate into behaviour. Make up a grid with the following headings: Facts, Opinions, Consequences. Transfer your thoughts on to the grid. For example:

Facts	Opinions	Consequences
I ate a bag of crisps	I'm a glutton	I abandoned my diet
My joke went down badly	I'm insensitive	I didn't ask for a second date

5. **Argue with yourself.** Look for alternative opinions. What is the case for the defence? What are the mitigating circumstances? Where are the

alternative interpretations? What is an exaggeration? For example: the dieter could remember
the last five days when he or she stuck to the
sensible eating plan. The man could remember
the jokes that his date did laugh about. Put the
alternative opinions on to your grid and add
some alternative possible consequences.

Facts	Opinions	Consequences
I ate a bag of crisps	I've stuck to my diet up to now	Keep going
	I will occasion-ally have slips	Build treats into my diet
My joke went down badly	She liked my other jokes	Phone her
	I need to think before telling a joke	Be more careful next time

Try to come up with as many different opinions
as possible as each will suggest another alternative
outcome and many of them will be optimistic.

Positive Thinking

Once the negative voices in your head have been cut down to size, you will find that there is a more positive one waiting to be heard. This is certainly the experience of Martina, with the lucky sisters, whom we met earlier in the chapter: 'I got caught up in a sales call at work, but I managed to get him off the phone in a couple of minutes. In the past, I'd have been angry with myself for wasting time but instead I thought "You handled that quite well".' It was not just her own voice that began to cut through the negative chatter, she also started to hear praise from her colleagues and seniors.

'What if that gremlin starts up again?' I asked.

'I'll tell him, there are three successful sisters in our family – not just two.'

Six months later, she contacted me with the news that she had transferred to another division – which brought her into contact with media, art and fashion companies as she'd always dreamed – and had gained a promotion too.

Summing Up

There are three kinds of negative thinking which work together to undermine your self-confidence. The good news is that progress in one area will help in the others. Challenging the beliefs that drive **limited thinking** will make you less likely to fall into the trap of **black-and-white thinking** and help you find a more balanced assessment of a problem. This in turn will make you less prone to **pessimistic thinking** where setbacks are all-pervasive, personal and permanent.

Finally, you are ready to listen to your more optimistic voice that says problems are temporary and down to specific circumstances, so therefore easier to overcome.

IN A NUTSHELL:

- Cut down negative thinking by challenging your automatic beliefs and finding if they are based on fact or just opinion.
- Check your language. Are you using black-and-white language like 'never' or 'always'? What would happen if you substituted 'sometimes' or 'on this occasion'?
- Take one of your positive beliefs about yourself and repeat it whenever your negative voice is getting the upper hand.

STEP 5

SET REALISTIC GOALS

In the last two steps we have covered how other people and our own inner voice can pull us down. There is a third force at play which undermines our self-esteem but it is more subtle and less obvious than the other two. One of the most significant changes in recent years has been the explosion in consumer choice. Where once we could opt for either butter or margarine, there are now low-fat spreads, low-salt, organic, buttermilks with added omega three or olive oil, no-hydrogenated oils and myriad other choices. Although making up our minds can be tough, we all buy into the mantra that choice is good.

Politicians offer more choice about where to send our children to school or at which hospital to have an operation, confident in the belief that this will get them elected. Certainly no choice means no control over our lives, no freedom and no personal autonomy; it would indeed be unbearable. However, Barry Schwartz, Professor of Social Theory and Social Action at Swarthmore College in the US, believes that unlimited choice is just as bad as no choice and could be at the root of our high levels of unhappiness, dissatisfaction and depression.

He got the idea for his groundbreaking book, *The Paradox of Choice* (HarperCollins, 2004), when he went to buy some jeans. He had worn out his old, favourite pair and simply wanted to replace them. Instead, he was offered easy fit, relaxed fit, baggy or extra baggy. Did he want them stone-washed, acid-washed or distressed? the assistant asked. While the professor looked at her blankly, she asked if he wanted zip or button fly and faded or regular. It is easy to laugh at an academic out of touch with fashion, but unlimited choice is turning more and more people into perfectionists and this is a fast track to self-hatred.

Why Less Really is More

In a laboratory study, students were asked to taste and rate a selection of gourmet chocolates. Half the students were given only six chocolates to eat while the other half were given thirty. Not only did the students with less choice rate their chocolates higher, but they were also four times as likely to choose chocolate, rather than cash, as a thank you for taking part in the research. So why were they more satisfied? Professor Schwartz believes that greater choice actually diminishes our enjoyment because we fear that amongst the discarded options is something that we might have liked more.

Not only does unlimited choice make it harder to choose, it makes us believe that somewhere there is the perfect product. Returning to Professor Schwartz's search for the jeans, the assistant conferred with her colleague to try and decide what he meant by regular jeans, 'you know, the kind that used to be the only kind', and pointed him in the right direction. So far so good, but Professor Schwartz began to wonder if one of the other options would be more comfortable, a better fit and ultimately look better on him. Somewhere in the piles of merchandise was a more desirable pair than the jeans in his hands. Previously when he had bought 'regular' jeans, they had become 'perfect' jeans as he wore the stiffness out of the fabric and they had given a little here and there and moulded to his body.

The same force is at play with modern relationships and it is making us increasingly dissatisfied. We would like to believe that somewhere there is the 'perfect' partner, a soulmate with whom we can live harmoniously for evermore. Unlike with the old-fashioned 'regular' partner, there will be no need for nasty rows or rough edges, but an immediate, magical union. Worse still, if we do not have the 'perfect' partner, we think there is something wrong with us. Somehow we are not beautiful, successful or interesting enough to be happy.

In reality, jeans and relationships have a lot in common. There is seldom an instant fit but, over time, we grow into both and before too long we would not wish to parted from either.

Maximisers and Satisfiers

In the fifties, Nobel Prize-winning economist Herbert Simon decided to look at how people coped with choice; even then consumers had a wide range of products, and big-ticket items – such as cars and washing machines – constituted a major investment. He found that the population divided into two categories the 'Maximiser' and the 'Satisfier'.

The Maximiser will settle only for the very best. When shopping, the Maximiser might find something that fulfils all his or her criteria – let's stay with jeans – but, instead of buying them in the first store, will hide them under the rest of the stock (heaven forbid that someone else should buy them). Next, the Maximiser sets off to try all the other shops in town, maybe returning and digging out the hidden pair. The Maximiser cannot purchase anything until he or she has looked at all the possibilities.

On one hand, it is great to aspire to the best, but there are always doubts. Even carrying home the prized purchase, the Maximiser has nagging worries: 'Maybe I should have tried one more store. What if I had travelled into a larger town?' If it was tough being a Maximiser in the fifties, it is even worse with the unlimited possibilities of the Internet. Today a Maximiser has more choice and even more stockists. He or she might have the right jeans but maybe someone, somewhere, is offering them more cheaply. Yet despite all the stress involved, the Maximiser believes anything less than perfect is settling for mediocrity.

Meanwhile, if a Satisfier found a good pair of jeans in the first store, he or she would weigh up the fit, quality and price but would choose quickly and decisively. If all his or her criteria were met, the Satisfier would purchase the jeans – end of story. It might be possible to buy the jeans more cheaply elsewhere but the Satisfier cannot be bothered to look. This is because a Satisfier aims for good rather than the *very* best.

Professor Schwartz is probably a Satisfier; he had never felt short-changed by just one type of jeans. However, his shopping trip made him question his old buying habits and started his journey to his book's conclusion: unlimited choice is turning more of us into Maximisers.

What's So Wrong With Wanting the Best?

In the last chapter, we met Sandy who had been divorced for six years and feared that she would never find love again. 'Of course I have high standards, but doing my very best helps me feel good about myself. What's wrong with that?' With truly important decisions, nobody says: 'I want a "good enough" school for my children' or 'a "good enough" doctor to treat my cancer'. We want the *best* school and the *best* doctor. When it comes to relationships, nobody wants to *settle* but, rather, to walk up the aisle with the *best* partner.

However, there is one problem: we might want the best, but how do we know when we have found it? For example, it might be possible to find the best fridge-freezer. We can consult, say, fifty websites and find the best price. After all, price is easily comparable. Except, we might also want energy efficiency; although this is a statistic that can be compared from one model to the next, how do we trade off the benefits of price with energy efficiency? There are other issues too: capacity, ice-making facilities, design. Although the calculation is hard, there are a limited number of variables to rank before making a purchase. But what about the best school? We can consult league tables, but what about the distance travelled, the after-school clubs, the personality of our child and the facilities in his or her area of interest? What about the personality of their form teacher? Their classmates? Not only are there unlimited variables but also each one is almost impossible to call. As for the best doctor, how can we even hope to judge?

So what about the best partner? Especially when searching online or speed-dating, how can we rank the possible choices? The problem is that maximising increases our tendency to judge on the external factors that can be ranked – such as looks, height, figure and wealth – rather than internal qualities like character, trustworthiness, openness and generosity, which cannot. However, these internal qualities are ultimately going to be the deciding factors on whether a relationship is a success or a failure.

Maximising also encourages us to compare – otherwise how do we know if we have the best deal? Certainly Sandy was very concerned about how her latest boyfriend would appear to her friends and, in particular, her sister: 'By some fluke, I met this guy who had a small part in this soap opera that my sister watched. You should have seen her face when we turned up to a family barbecue.' I was already suspicious that Sandy was a Maximiser and perfectionist. 'I really wiped the smile off her self-satisfied face,' said Sandy. 'At times like that it really makes up for all those dud dates, when I'm spending boring hours with losers in pubs.'

However, while Maximising might stop someone for 'settling' for second best, it also makes commitment harder as choosing to walk up the aisle with one person automatically excludes all the other potentially better lovers. By contrast, Satisfiers have more trust in their own judgement.

They are aiming for 'good enough' and each person will have their own way of measuring this. For this reason, a Satisfier has less reason to compare their beloved. Spending less time looking over his or her shoulder, a Satisfier is more likely to be contented with their partner and therefore find it easier to settle down. So what happened with Sandy and her boyfriend? Did they find happiness and love together? 'Sadly, he turned out to like his booze too much and when he'd had a lot to drink, he started flirting with other women,' she explained.

Maximisers are also more likely to aspire to dating outside their league. The most beautiful woman or handsomest man might seem like a highway to happiness but we also increase our risk of being rejected. The comic writer and actor Harvey Fierstein has an amusing take on this phenomenon. In his award-winning play *Torch Song Trilogy*, his lead character advises: 'An ugly person who goes after a pretty person gets nothing but trouble. But a pretty person who goes after an ugly person gets at least a cab fare.'

The final problem with maximising is that it is often a cover for low self-esteem. 'I feel good about myself if I'm on the arm of a handsome man,' said Sandy, later in her counselling, 'because unless I go for the very best, I feel entirely worthless and useless – like the lint you get out of the tumble drier. Just throw it away.' Like many coping strategies, maximising was making Sandy's self-worth much lower because aiming for perfection, all of the time, set her up for failure and another round of self-hatred.

MAXIMISER/SATISFIER SCALE

You can find out whether you are a Maximiser or a Satisfier by taking the following test. Score your level of agreement with each statement on a scale of one to five. Five means that you completely agree with the statement, one means that you completely disagree and three means that you are neutral.

1. At parties, I find myself looking over the shoulder of the person that I'm talking to – even during interesting chats – in case I'm missing something.

2. Dating is rather like clothes shopping. I expect to try on a lot before finding the perfect fit.

3. With television, I often flip through the other channels even though I'm watching something else.

4. I am not keen on committing to a night out with friends too far into the future, in case a better offer comes up.

5. After going shopping, I often feel less positive about my purchases when I get home.

6. I worry that other people get a better deal. On holiday, I like to find out how much other guests paid or avoid such conversations because I'm worried that others paid less and I will feel bad about myself.

7. When driving somewhere, I can stress myself out by wondering if there is less traffic on another route or whether I should have taken a train or some other form of transport.

8. I often find myself thinking, what would have happened if I had made different choices? Such as studying something different or not breaking up with someone.

9. No matter what, I have the highest standards for myself.

10. I find Christmas stressful because it's important to find the right gifts for everybody.

11. On Monday morning, when everybody is talking about their weekends, I often worry that other people have a better time, funnier friends or a nicer family.

12. When my insurance comes up for renewal, I will normally consult at least ten alternative quotes.

13. I like to find out how things turned out for old boyfriends or girlfriends.

14. I find it hard to make my mind up in restaurants and when other people's food arrives, I often feel they ordered more wisely.

Add up your points and discover where you fit on the scale.

Under thirty-five

You are a Satisfier. If you find something that works, you are likely to stick with it, whether it is a brand of toothpaste or a song on the car radio (a Maximiser would channel-hop in case another station was playing a better song). When it comes to shopping, you consider a manageable number of options and settle for something that fits the bill – rather than the best possible item. As a Satisfier, you are less likely to suffer buyer's remorse because your identity is not tied up with finding the perfect product at the best price possible.

However, there is a balance between not getting stressed out by choice and taking the easy way out. Many businesses make their profits out of Satisfiers who stay, for example, on the same mortgage rate for years, while the Maximisers have long since switched to a lower rate. You need to be certain that when it comes to the important areas of your life – job, relationships and family – you are not just settling for a quiet life. By maximising in these areas, you could get a promotion or more out of your relationships – rather than let people take advantage and walk all over you.

Thirty-five to forty-five

Most people fit somewhere in the middle of the Maximiser and Satisfier scale. In some areas you will aim for the best, and in others you will settle for good enough. This is called 'domain specific' maximising. For example, you might care passionately about fine wines and look for the perfect bottle to accompany a meal but are unlikely to keep switching Internet providers in search of the best deal. When it comes to key areas, like work and relationships, you want to do your best but have realistic expectations of what is possible. By contrast, a Maximiser has not only high standards but expects always to achieve them. As this is impossible, a Maximiser can end up disappointed, depressed and ultimately demotivated. Be aware that unlimited choice, and clever marketing, are putting pressure on all of us to tip towards the maximising end of the scale. So do not be tempted to consider more than a manageable number of alternatives – probably around six – as unlimited choice often makes for worse rather than better decisions.

Forty-six plus

You are a Maximiser. You never settle for second best and this means that you take a while to come to a decision. In theory, you should be the person most likely to be pleased with your choices – except you are often filled with regret. Even if a decision turns out well, you will be disappointed if another option turned out better still. The higher your score, the most likely you are to assess missed opportunities: the job turned down, the holiday not taken, the boyfriend or girlfriend that got away.

It is fine to have high standards for yourself, but it is better to concentrate on a few key areas (such as job, personal morality and particular interests) than expect to excel in everything. Finally, try not to compare yourself to other people as this will increase dissatisfaction with your own life. There will always be people ahead but even if life is a competition – which I doubt – it is better to take a long view. This will help you see all your achievements – not just one disappointment. Ultimately, you will have a less stressful life if you let go of best and aim for attainable.

Reset Your Maximiser Thermometer

If unlimited choice is turning us all into Maximisers, it is important to concentrate on a few areas to maximise – otherwise we risk becoming overloaded, exhausted and frustrated. The following exercise is aimed at your purchasing decisions – especially for small-ticket items. Changing your attitude to inconsequential purchases will not only free up more time and energy for important choices but also offer a chance to experiment with being a Satisfier. This is important because committed Maximisers find it hardest to love themselves enough.

1. Look back at your last significant purchase.
   - How many websites did you consider?
   - How many shops did you visit?
   - What else went into making the decision?

2. Calculate the costs.
   - How long did it take to make your mind up? Even if it is an estimate, put down a figure.
   - How much money did you save? Be realistic with this figure. Instead of the difference between the highest quote and the eventual price, take the saving achieved by maximising – above and beyond that of a regular careful shopper.

3. How satisfied were you with the purchase?
   - Did you have any buyer's regret?
   - Did your effort provide more, less or about the same pleasure as someone investing less time and energy?

4. Did the effort involved justify maximising on this purchase?

- Think about how much an hour of your time is worth. (If you are self-employed, you will probably have an hourly rate. If you work for someone else, make a rough estimate by breaking down your salary into a daily and then an hourly rate.)
- Compare this figure with the saving achieved by maximising.
- Was maximising a good investment of your time or energy?

5. Set yourself an artificial constraint.
   - Take three quotes only.
   - Consider only six websites.
   - Look in only two shops.
   - Give yourself only half an hour.
   - The exact constraint is up to you and might change from purchase to purchase. However, set the limit in advance and stick to it.

6. Reassess your purchasing patterns.
   - What were the differences when you satisfied rather than maximised?
   - Did it work out better? If so, in what way?
   - How could you incorporate the benefits into other parts of your life?

7. Make a pact with yourself.
   - Resist the temptations laid out by the advertising industry. If something really is 'new and improved' your friends will probably recommend it.
   - Compare down rather than up. The lifestyles of the rich and famous will always make you feel inadequate. Instead, compare yourself with your contemporaries or, better still, people less fortunate.
   - Aim for good enough rather than perfect.

The Art of Setting Goals

Goals are a double-edged sword. Without them, we have a tendency to drift through life, muddling along, and are likely to wake one morning wondering where the last ten years went. However, a list of goals unmet can severely undermine our self-esteem. Worse still, if a goal is too low, there is no satisfaction in achieving it and only the illusion of progress. If a goal is so high that it is almost impossible, then we set ourselves up for failure.

One of the themes running through this book is finding the middle path. Not thinking that you're wonderful, nor thinking that you're terrible – but loving yourself enough. This is why this step is about setting **realistic** goals.

Ask yourself the following questions:

1. What am I hoping to achieve?
2. By when?
3. How will I know when I've got there?
4. Do I really need it? (Is this someone else's dream? Am I still trying to be a perfectionist and only accepting the very best outcome?)
5. What small step could I take towards my goal?

As we head into the final section of my programme, the following exercise will not only help you take stock of your progress so far but also help you begin to set realistic goals:

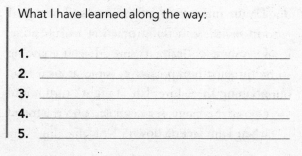

What I have learned along the way:

1. _____
2. _____
3. _____
4. _____
5. _____

One change I can make:

_____

What I need:

1. _____
2. _____
3. _____

What I should avoid:

1. _____
2. _____
3. _____

Some notes on goal-setting:

- Do not feel constrained by the numbers in the exercise above. They are just a guideline.
- Try to make your answer to 'one change I can make' something practical and positive, for example, 'learn to sing'. If you come up with something negative, for example, 'stop phoning an ex-lover late at night', turn it into a positive change, for example, 'phone a friend when I am feeling down'.

- Your 'one change' might seem small, in comparison with the needs, but remember **one** small change can set up lots of other positive changes that will lead to a happy and fulfilling life.

- Be wary of huge changes. There is always the danger of going for the opposite of your current behaviour. Unfortunately, this will preserve the problem, as it did with Sandy, who swung between being jealous and being the object of her boyfriend's jealousy, and ended up playing the opposing role in the same drama.

- With bigger goals, set smaller sub-goals along the way.

- Think ahead. What would help you overcome obstacles? What rewards could you give yourself?

- Be prepared to explore alternative outcomes and enjoy the journey. Having too rigid a destination sets you up for disappointment and downgrades the opportunities found along the way.

To help you get started, here are the answers that Sandy and I created together:

What I have learned along the way:

1. I never really knew my father.
2. I am resourceful.
3. With help, I can overcome big obstacles. (She had counselling to get her drinking under control.)
4. I can be generous.

One change I can make:

Help out at a local theatre society that works with disabled and able-bodied children. (Volunteering is a great way to boost self-esteem.)

What I need:

1. To get to know a man before falling in love.

What I should avoid:

1. Controlling men.
2. Men who idolise me and will put up with any behaviour.

Summing Up

Modern marketing techniques and unlimited consumer choice have made us dissatisfied not only with the products on sale in the shops but also with ourselves. Maximisers are more likely to compare themselves with other people. This increases the chance of them feeling negative about themselves and their choice of partner. Satisfiers find it easier to choose, because they are aiming for a good enough product rather than the best one. They find it easier to make a relationship, but risk 'settling' and becoming trapped in unfulfilling relationships. The answer is to aim to be somewhere in between these two extremes.

IN A NUTSHELL:

- Being a perfectionist is undermining your self-esteem.
- Compare yourself less with other people.
- Keep asking yourself: Do I really want this? Am I marching to someone else's drum? Am I at risk of setting myself an unrealistic goal?

STEP

6

REBALANCE YOURSELF

How we feel about ourselves has a major impact on how other people feel about us. If we consider ourselves to be OK, somebody whose opinions should be listened to and taken into consideration, then other people will treat us in this way too. If we consider ourselves unworthy and unimportant, other people will disregard us or take us for granted. In effect, feeling good enough about ourselves can transform all of our relationships. However, this transformation has to be more than just on the surface. Other people have in-built detectors which let them know if confidence is put on and if we are demanding respect which we do not feel we truly deserve.

In order to help you probe deeply and work on hidden opinions about yourself, I need to help you find a way down to your unconscious. This is easier if approached at an angle, rather than head-on, so the next section might seem odd, but be patient.

Stories and the Unconscious

From the beginning of time, mankind has been fascinated by stories not just as entertainment but as a way to make sense of the world. What is most extraordinary is that the oldest-surviving story – discovered by the explorer Henry Layard in 1839 on clay tablets under a mound of sand in the desert of Mesopotamia – would be instantly recognised today. 'The Epic of Gilgamesh' is about a society threatened by a great evil. The source is traced to a distant underground cavern and the hero, Gilgamesh, arms himself with a mighty axe and sets off to save mankind. Although this story was found in the remains of one of the earliest cities built by mankind, we are still watching it today at our local multiplex – for example, as the latest James Bond.

So what has all this got to do with loving your-self enough? There are two important insights. As every culture, throughout all time, has told the same stories, these plots offer an extraordinary insight into what it means to be human and the problems we face. (I will go on to explore this idea further in a moment.) The second insight is that as soon as we are old enough to focus on pictures and understand words, we are told stories by our parents. We are introduced to the world around us through stories and remain mesmerised for the rest of our lives. And it is not just movies, books and television drama; documentary makers, historians, journalists and the producers of 'reality shows' are all using the same building blocks to help us process millions of disparate and often contradictory bits of information into one coherent and compelling narrative.

This is why understanding the stories that we tell ourselves, and others, is a direct route to our unconscious.

Seven Basic Plot Lines

Although millions of books have been written and thousands of films and television programmes have been made, there are actually only a handful of different permutations. These are set out by Christopher Booker in his groundbreaking book *The Seven Basic Plots* (Continuum, 2004). So what are they?

1. Overcoming the monster

Ordinary life comes under a terrible shadow. A young hero emerges who overcomes extraordinary odds, defeats the monster and becomes a wiser, stronger and more mature person. Society as a whole has benefited and everyone is safe again.

Examples: *Jaws, Star Wars, Jack & the Beanstalk*.

Who might use this plot: Someone who has come out the other side of a damaging relationship or an addiction problem (where the monster is in some way their own behaviour).

2. Rags to riches

An ordinary person, dismissed by everyone else, takes centre stage and is revealed to be someone very special. This is perhaps one of the most popular plots.

Examples: *Cinderella, Pretty Woman* (in effect, Cinderella for the 1990s), *Cocktail* (this Tom Cruise movie puts a man into the Cinderella role), *The Ugly Duckling, Aladdin* or *Jane Eyre*.

Who might use this plot: Anyone who feels that love will transform their lives but is waiting for someone to come along and raise them up or inspire them.

3. The quest

A hero learns of a priceless goal, worth any effort to achieve. He or she leaves home and sets off on a perilous journey. Whatever happens on the way, whatever distractions, the story cannot be resolved until he or she reaches the goal.

Examples: *Lord of the Rings*, *The Odyssey*, *The Da Vinci Code.*

Who might use this plot: Anyone who has been trying to gain self-respect – the ultimate priceless goal in many stories – rather than waiting for someone to 'save' them.

4. Voyage and return

Rather than deliberately setting off on a quest, the hero finds himself or herself in a strange world and has many thrilling adventures, but eventually decides to return home again. Generally, the hero has not been outwardly changed by their adventures.

Examples: *Alice in Wonderland* (Alice falls down the rabbit hole and later wakes up and considers it all a dream), *The Wizard of Oz* (Dorothy is blown to Oz by a hurricane but does at least learn that there is 'no place like home'), *Gone with the Wind*, *Around the World in Eighty Days*.

Who might use this plot: Someone who has been on a lot of exciting or horrifying dates but remains basically the same person.

5. Comedy

This is a particular plot – not just a funny story – and is instantly recognisable today as the genre of movie called 'romantic comedy'. The roots, however, go all the way back to Greek drama. Two true lovers are separated by either circumstances (traditionally parents who disapprove of the union) or misunderstandings between the lovers. Things go from bad to worse and it seems the lovers will never come together. At the last moment, the obstacles are overcome and not only are the couple united but also their families and their community celebrate.

Examples: The books of Jane Austen (who revolutionised the genre by introducing the idea that the obstacle might partly be the character of the heroine, not just outside forces), *The Importance of Being Earnest, Some Like it Hot, Notting Hill, My Big Fat Greek Wedding.*

Who might use this plot: Anyone whose love story has hit a stumbling block will look for ways to overcome the obstacles created by other people or the misunderstandings arising from not truly knowing each other's feelings.

6. Tragedy

This plot has been called comedy with an unhappy ending, and the shape of the two story types are remarkably similar. In both plots, a wider society is under a shadow because someone is thinking only about themselves and their own needs or opinions. In tragedy, it is normally the hero or heroine who is causing the problem. He or she has some good qualities but also a fatal flaw that makes him or her follow their own needs at the expense of everyone else. Although things might go well for a while, eventually the obstacles get greater and greater. Unlike in comedy, these problems are not overcome. The hero fails to learn or change until it is too late and meets an unhappy end (normally death). However, society learns something and is cleansed by the experience.

Examples: *Othello* (there are many of the misunderstandings of a traditional comedy in *Othello* – such as dropped handkerchiefs – but they are not resolved and the hero murders the heroine), *Madame Bovary*, *Anna Karenina*, *Bonnie & Clyde*.

Who might use this plot: Anyone who gets a perverse pleasure out of a doomed love affair and certainly falling for a married man/woman follows this plot with the heroine/hero nearly always ending up alone.

7. Rebirth

A dark shadow has been cast over the hero. For a while, danger might be comfortably remote but eventually it consumes everything, until the hero is almost experiencing a living death. However, at the very last moment, the hero is redeemed by someone traditionally considered less powerful – perhaps a child, an old man or a woman, and everybody lives happily ever after.

Examples: *A Christmas Carol* (Scrooge is saved by his compassion for Tiny Tim), *Beauty and the Beast, Sleeping Beauty, The Snow Queen, Charlie and the Chocolate Factory.*

Who might use this plot: Someone who wants to save their beloved – normally from themselves, but more likely bad habits, debt or emotional problems.

In effect, stories present us with a guide to what it means to be human, an explanation of how and why our neighbours behave like they do, and a set of rules for everybody to live together. We have heard these stories so many times that they have been programmed into our unconscious in a way that we cannot modify or control. Our choice of plot lines, however, will depend on our particular perspective. The woman who has fallen in love with a married man might look at events through the lens of 'Rebirth'. Her beloved is under the spell of a witch who does not truly love her husband and is therefore ruining his life. She has come along to redeem him and make him truly happy. Meanwhile, the wife would probably view events through 'Overcoming the monster', with the mistress cast as the monster. The husband might initially be in 'Comedy' and certainly many farces are focused on a man trying to keep his wife and mistress apart. However, from the perspective of people outside the triangle, it will probably be a 'Tragedy'. So look over the seven plots and think about your own autobiography. Did you ever feel that you were living out a story? If so, which ones? There is more about this below.

STORIES IN ACTION

If you keep on seeing the same plot line – over and over – or you expect love to conform to one in particular, this is a useful insight into your subconscious.

Identify your personal plot

There are two ways of approaching this part of the exercise:

First, look at books, films or stories that have really moved you. For example, my favourites include: *The*

Shipping News by Annie Proulx (Rebirth: Bereaved man and his family leave New York for the land of their forefathers – a remote frozen part of Newfoundland); *The Curious Incident of the Dog in the Night-time* by Mark Haddon (Quest: Fifteen-year-old boy with Asperger's syndrome sets off on a journey to find his mother); and *Promise of Happiness* by Justin Cartwright (Rebirth: Daughter comes out of prison after serving a sentence for art theft and her family emerges from the shadow of the crisis).

As I'm a therapist, it is not surprising that my tastes reflect my interest in change and people discovering something important about themselves. However, until I did this exercise myself, I had not been aware how my favourites had such similar themes. What do your favourite stories tell you about yourself?

Second, look at your own life. Imagine that you are going to write your own autobiography. What would you call it? Which of the Seven Basic Plots would dominate? Looking at the beginning of your autobiography, what would be the chapter headings? What major events would be covered? Imagining that each of these events would be given a whole chapter, what would that chapter be called? You might even like to get a few pieces of paper, put the title of your autobiography on the first and then write out the chapter headings. What kind of stories do you tell yourself to make sense of your life?

Understand what these stories say about you

Below are the Seven Basic Plots and some suggestions about what each plot might be trying to teach you – especially if your autobiography, or one of the chapters in it, conforms to the storyline.

Overcoming the monster: The most important question to ask yourself is: Have I overcome all the monsters? In many movies using this theme, there are often several minor monsters before the main adversary. For example, in *King Kong*, the heroine is threatened by several dinosaurs before facing her greatest threat: Kong at the top of the Empire State Building. Real-life problems often come in packs too and we need to work our way through destructive coping strategies to reach the real enemy underneath. An example would be Hannah, thirty-seven, who tackled a nasty drink problem: 'I would do stupid, dangerous things like going out drinking, falling asleep on the Tube and being woken by the guard at the end of the line. It would be so late that the underground had stopped and I'd be forced to get a taxi home.'

Hannah undertook a treatment programme and made great progress. 'That's when my old eating disorder came back with a vengeance and I started stuffing myself with cheap cakes from the corner store,' she explained. 'The problem had begun when I was a kid – I'd peel the wallpaper off my bedroom wall and suck on it.' She was finally ready to talk about the abuse she suffered at the hands of her older brother. If this is your plot, celebrate your past achievements – and the monsters slain – but be realistic about the challenges ahead.

Rags to riches: The problem with this plot is that the hero or heroine can be waiting to be lifted up – normally by a prince or princess – rather than finding a way to lift themselves up from the shadows. Even in movies like *Flashdance* (a welder wants a place at an exclusive dance academy) where the heroine is developing a skill to gain recognition, the plot line glosses over the sheer number of hours needed and there is normally a love interest who opens the door to success. (In *Flashdance* the welder's boss uses his contacts to get her the crucial audition.) Talent shows, like *The X Factor* and *Pop Idol*, work on the 'Rags to riches' plot too. However, the producers always omit important facts – such as the winning contestants have been taking singing lessons since they were five years old – so that the audience can relate to the 'ordinary' boy or girl who finds fame. This might make good television, but misleads people into waiting to be discovered. If this is your favourite plot, ask yourself: What can I do to make things happen for myself? Am I repeating old patterns – same job, same friends, going to the same places – but expecting new things to happen? How can I change?

Quest: This is a very positive plot line. The hero has a clear goal, expects obstacles and setbacks, but is not put off. Unlike 'Voyage and return' – see below – he or she learns something important during the quest and the reader/audience feel that they have deserved to reach the goal. If your favourite books and movies use this plot, congratulate yourself as this suggests that you are a positive and upbeat person. If a chapter of your autobiography fits this plot, look back at what skills, qualities and strategies helped you reach your goal.

Voyage and return: When swapping disastrous date stories with friends, you are often conforming to this plot. In other words, you have been to a strange world and seen strange things but have decided to return home. Although you might have learned something from the experience, it is usually superficial. For example, don't wear high heels when dancing with short men.

Don't worry if this seems to be your auto-biography or a couple of chapters of it, as everybody goes through this stage in the journey from adolescence to adulthood. The secret is to turn 'Voyage and return' into 'Quest' and to learn something important from your experiences. So think back to one of your date stories – in par-ticular, one that is critical of the other person – and ask yourself: What does this story say about me? For example, in the dancing-with-a-short-guy story: Do I make snap judgements on superficial qualities without knowing the real person? Are you attributing someone else's bad behaviour to a character flaw, but the same behaviour in your-self to particular circumstances. For example, when someone else shouts, they are short-tempered; when you shout, you are provoked or temporarily in a bad mood.

Comedy: Hollywood has used this story so many times that we know within minutes who will fall for whom. The interest is in seeing how they overcome the obstacles and find true love. However, few filmgoers stop and question the shape of this plot – which shows just how deeply ingrained into our subconscious it is. So how exactly has the comedy plot influenced our picture of love?

The answer is best summed up with a line from *A Midsummer Night's Dream* – one of Shakespeare's most performed comedies: 'The course of true love never did run smooth.' In other words, we have been trained to expect problems but know that 'love conquers all' (Virgil, 70–19 BC). The result is we believe that not only can we fall for someone totally unsuitable but also that love will smooth over the problems, resolve our differences and provide a happy ending. Worse still, we can put up with bad behaviour from a new lover – rudeness, abusive language or even contempt – because many couples in romantic movies start off hating each other. If this is your favourite plot, or your previous love affairs have followed the first part of the comedy plot, ask yourself: Do I expect too much from love? Love might be magical but it cannot magic away problems.

Tragedy: When we have had a few drinks, it is easy to become melancholic and view ourselves as a tragic hero or heroine. So that, in the words of one of the greatest of Shakespeare's tragic characters, King Lear, we are: 'more sinned against than sinning'. In other words, we might have done something wrong – like sleeping with a married man or woman – but actually we are the victim of a more serious wrong. The whole world is against us.

Although this strategy can make us feel better in the short term, it can also stop us from properly acknowledging our mistakes, our own part in our misery and learning something beneficial for the future. In some cases, I find that people with tragic autobiographies have cast themselves in too dark a light. An example would be Molly – a twenty-eight-year-old single mother with a twelve-year-old son. When she was young she had babysat for the children of her father's best friend. 'I had always been very close to this man – he'd been like an honorary uncle – and I'd been having a bad time at school. He listened, and you can guess the rest. Well, it broke my father's heart when he found out. I tried to keep my pregnancy secret; I guess I was in denial. Dad had been in the Navy with this guy, they went right back, and it ruined their friendship. The man and his wife ended up getting divorced too. How could I have been so selfish?' I had to remind Molly that she had been underage and slowly she accepted that not all the blame was hers. Eventually, she changed her plot to 'Overcoming the monster'. Would this be helpful for you too?

Rebirth: This is another positive plot as it involves someone changing and casting off dark shadows. However, unlike 'Rags to riches', the hero or heroine does the majority of the work themselves. So if you enjoy this plot in books or films, or you see your autobiography as being under a dark shadow, how can you use the lessons and reach your own rebirth? Time and again in rebirth stories, the hero or heroine is very isolated. Scrooge has no friends and keeps his nephew at a distance. Mary in *The Secret Garden* is an orphan sent to a remote mansion on the Yorkshire moors. Look at your own life: why are you isolated? What could be done to change it? The other common thread through 'Rebirth' is seeing the problem through fresh eyes. For Scrooge it is the visit from the three ghosts and for Mary it is the arrival of spring. How could you find a fresh perspective on your life? Remember, you are not looking for someone to turn your life around but for something to provide the impetus for you to do it yourself.

Becoming Balanced

If stories provide a guide on how to live, by analysing what heroes need at the beginning of a story, what they gain through their adventures and why some stories turn into tragedy, we can learn what makes the good life. So what are the lessons coded into all stories?

1. At the beginning of every story, the hero lacks something.
2. The hero is in some way unbalanced.
3. In a 'Comedy', what the hero lacks is in some way represented by the heroine. He has to learn her value so that they can be united and become one balanced whole.
4. In a 'Tragedy', the hero keeps on becoming more and more unbalanced until nothing can save him/her. The hero ends up alone or dead.
5. In 'Quest' and 'Overcoming the monster', the prized object, defeating evil or lessons learned on the journey will balance the hero.
6. In 'Rags to riches' and 'Rebirth', the hero emerges from the shadows and either society or the hero himself/herself has a more balanced view.

7. The story ends happily when everyone, and society in general, has reached balance.

So what do I mean by balance? This is where I need to bring in the theories of Carl Jung, one of the founding fathers of psychology, who studied myths and legends and believed that, like dreams, they offer an insight into the dark corners of our minds. Jung concluded that a happy and fulfilled person is in touch with two very different parts of their psyche: the animus (inward-looking) and the anima (outward-looking).

Animus	Anima
Strong	Compassionate
Disciplined	Intuitive
Self-controlled	Sensitive to the needs of others
Firm	Understanding
Rational	Able to see the whole picture

Traditionally, the qualities associated with animus have been seen as masculine strengths and those of anima as feminine ones. However, it goes without saying that men can be sensitive and women can be rational. This is the genius of Jung: rather than falling in with the prevailing stereotypes at the beginning of the twentieth century, he believed that both genders had to be in touch with both sets of qualities to achieve balance.

REBALANCING THE ANIMUS AND ANIMA

1. What is the bigger picture?

- Start with your own natural reaction to an important event in your life. Does it tend towards the animus or the anima?

- If tipping towards animus, look at whether the short-term benefits of being self-orientated (for example, getting your own way) might be outweighed by the long-term benefits of considering others (such as, better cooperation with colleagues). If tipping towards anima, although there are short-term benefits in always putting others first (for example, it makes you feel good about yourself or keeps the peace), what are the longer-term downsides (perhaps, being taken for granted)?

2. Work outwards

(This is only for people tipping towards the animus; if you tip towards the anima, go to part three.)

- What are the needs of other people? How are they impacted by your behaviour?
- What about the community in general?
- What would be the consequences if everybody behaved like you?

3. Walk a mile in someone else's shoes

- Imagine you are a friend or a family member who is close enough to be affected by your behaviour.
- What would be their opinion of your behaviour?
- How do they feel?
- Still in their shoes: how would you judge your own behaviour?

4. What could you do differently next time?

- With your fresh perspective, think about the changes that you would like to make.
- If you are stuck for an idea, try the opposite of your normal approach.

- This is bound to help you experience the opposite part of your psyche.

5. Afterwards, analyse the changes
- What felt good?
- What felt uncomfortable but manageable?
- How could you build on this for the future?

Improving Your Relationship With Yourself and Others

Stories demonstrate the problems that arise when people become unbalanced. For example, tragic heroes are gripped by the animus part of their psyche and are so obsessed with their own needs that they are unaware of the chaos that they are spreading. Othello is consumed with jealousy and so overly rational (animus) that he can't see the false logic presented by his rival Iago, who is feeding him lies about his wife. With the animus firmly in control, Othello is so shut off from his anima (able to see the whole picture) that he can't recognise those qualities in Desdemona either. Therefore, Othello can't achieve balance and the play ends with a pile of dead bodies.

In a story with a happy ending, like *Beauty and the Beast*, the strength, discipline and self-control of the Beast is trapped until Beauty arrives with her compassion, understanding and the other qualities associated with the anima. At the beginning of *Pride and Prejudice*, Elizabeth is too in touch with her animus (rational and self-controlled) and therefore unable to access her anima (compassion). Therefore, she unfairly judges Mr Darcy, who is awkward in social situations and therefore not at his best at the ball. In all these stories, balance is finally achieved and everybody can live happily ever after.

It is all very well for Jung to say that we should be in touch with both animus and anima, but many of the virtues are contradictory. How can you be rational *and* intuitive or firm *and* sensitive? Indeed, throughout myths, legends and popular movies, there are few characters who start out balanced: Merlin in Arthurian legend; Gandalf in the *Lord of the Rings*; Athene, the goddess of wisdom, in *The Odyssey*. Interestingly, these are all solitary characters who have no need for another half because they are already complete. It is difficult for ordinary mortals to balance the qualities of anima and animus, so we have traditionally 'projected' the anima on to women and the animus on to men.

Returning to the specific issue of loving yourself enough to have a good relationship with yourself and others, stories tell us that we need a partner to feel complete and to become balanced. Think how many fairy tales, myths and legends end with a wedding – symbolising the coming together of the anima and animus. Stories also point out where someone unbalanced might be going wrong.

Starting with men, Martyn is a thirty-two-year-old whom I counselled about a string of intense relationships that ultimately went nowhere. When we looked at the patterns, we saw that he fell for women who were very needy. 'Their lives are often a mess and I can see what should be done and sort everything out. But although they are grateful, the relationship always fizzles out and turns into a friendship,' he explained. In effect, Martyn was so compassionate, intuitive and understanding – in touch with his anima – that he was unbalanced and at an unconscious level his girlfriends felt that he had nothing more to offer.

Another man who found it hard to make relationships was Luke, twenty-eight: 'I've come to the conclusion that women prefer bastards to nice guys.' In counselling, I quickly discovered that he was so anxious to please and sensitive to the needs of the women he dated that he found it hard to articulate what he wanted. 'I'd much rather do what pleases them.' I knew from my female clients that this is fine, up to a point, but makes it hard to get to know the real man and, worse still, women consider this behaviour 'weak' and therefore unattractive. Once again, Luke was too in touch with the anima side of his psyche. Other men with this dilemma include those who are too close to their mothers or divorcees who become over-bonded with their daughters. In both these examples, the men have achieved a sort of balance with the anima – except it is a twisted, dark version that is ultimately unhealthy.

Turning to women, what happens if they are too connected to one side of their psyche? A woman who is controlled by her anima will become too considerate, too compassionate and so sensitive to the needs of her man that she will put up with even abusive or disrespectful behaviour and could end up trapped in an unhappy marriage. If these women had strength, firmness and rationality (animus), they would walk away. In contrast, many women who have been single for a long time are unbalanced towards the animus.

Certainly, Karen, thirty-eight, came across as hard, brittle and a little self-obsessed when I interviewed her. She told me about a relationship with Brian, a long-distance lorry driver whom she'd been dating for three months, which ended on his birthday: 'I hadn't seen him for a week because he'd been delivering in Europe. I'd fixed a birthday supper, candles – the whole thing – but when I met him at the door with a kiss, he grabbed my boobs. I was fuming. I had a nice evening planned and he just seemed to want sex.' Karen had a very fixed idea of how Brian was going to spend his birthday: starting with a glass of champagne with a strawberry inside – 'I thought we could slip them into each other's mouths' – followed by light conversation about his trip with their starter, her news over the main course, then he would open his present before dessert and they would glide magically towards the bedroom. This determination to be in control and the discipline not to skip straight to love-making – Karen did find Brian very sexy – is typical animus. If she had been more in touch with her anima, she might have considered Brian's wishes – after all, it was his birthday. She might also have seen the bigger picture: he had spent a week on the road and had probably missed her terribly. Instead, Karen was so furious about her ruined plans that she picked a row and Brian stormed out without his present.

HOW BALANCED ARE YOU?

This is a good point in the journey towards loving yourself to check whether you have a balanced attitude. So ask yourself:

- Do I strive for excellence but avoid the trap of perfectionism?
- Can I find the right level of pressure to succeed without tipping over into avoidance or paralysis?
- Do I accept myself as I am but still remain aware of areas for future growth?

Next look at the balance between different areas of your life: work, relationships, home, health and hobbies/pastimes/sports. Ask yourself:

- Am I concentrating on one or two areas to the detriment of others?
- Do I get all my self-worth from one particular area – such as work or family – which makes me particularly vulnerable to redundancy or the children leaving home?

- Am I working too many hours or is modern communication eating into my private life so that work is a background hum wherever I am?
- Have the demands of family and other people crowded out everything else in my life?
- What place does recreation play in my life?
- Is there something important that I have left on the back burner?
- Could an increased emphasis on health and recreation improve my body image, reduce stress and improve stamina?

If your life feels out of balance, finish off by asking:

- What changes do I need to make?
- What resources do I have?
- Where could I get help?
- How could I make the journey easier by breaking it down into a series of smaller and more manageable parts?

Summing Up

Stories are like dreams: an express way to our unconscious. So understanding what types of stories you tell and which ones you like will unlock your secret love agenda. Stories also show the importance of rebalancing your life, so that you listen to your own needs but are still aware of the competing needs of other people.

IN A NUTSHELL:
- Problems lurk in the extremes; the middle way is the most successful way.
- If you are single, what kind of person would help balance you up?
- If you are in a relationship, how balanced does it feel?

STEP 7

CONQUER FEARS AND SETBACKS

The first six steps of my programme will help you to understand why you suffer from low self-esteem, make peace with the past and re-examine your attitudes. A lot of this work involves making an internal shift. However, loving yourself enough is also about overcoming the day-to-day problems that life and other people throw at us. The final step looks at some of these challenges and how to find a way round them.

Margery, fifty-two, made good progress through my programme. She had started counselling because she felt her husband of thirty years, David, undermined her confidence. So she was surprised when, in step one, we looked back to her childhood and how being sexually abused by a friend of the family affected her self-esteem. Next, in step two, Let Go of the Past, Margery acknowledged that she was still angry with herself and her parents:

'It makes no sense. How were they to know what was happening? I was too ashamed to tell them, because I knew they'd be devastated.'

'Why are you angry with yourself?' I asked.

'This doesn't make any sense either. I was only ten. How was I to know what to do? We didn't cover it at school and if we did, it was "don't talk to strangers" and he wasn't a stranger.'

I asked if Margery could forgive herself and her parents and she started crying, but they were cathartic tears. During step three, Don't Let Other People Run You Down, we looked at Margery's relationship with David. She realised that she had to take her share of the responsibility for their unhappy marriage: 'David took control because I was so unsure of myself. I might not have agreed with everything he did and said but I didn't stand up for myself.' After step four – Reprogramme Your Inner Voice – Margery discovered that she had a 'guardian voice', as well as a negative one, during an argument over their daughter. 'He'd use this "stop being so silly" tone of voice when I worried about her fitting in at university. It was like he was completely trampling over my feelings. But my guardian voice would say something like, "Don't let David get away with that" or "That's not right, say something."' She was surprised when David apologised. 'I told him that tone was old David and I didn't want him back, thank you.'

With step five, Set Realistic Goals, rather than trying to change their marriage overnight, Margery and David went away for a long weekend to celebrate their wedding anniversary. (They hadn't been away – just the two of them – since their children had been born.) And they took up ballroom dancing so that they could spend more quality time together.

Before long, their marriage was more balanced – step six – and if Margery didn't like something, she regularly spoke up. However, she still had a range of day-to-day fears, including driving on her own, going out on her own and shopping alone. So how could she tackle these fears?

The Fear Trap

Low self-esteem has a lot to do with fear: fear of making a fool of yourself, fear of being exposed as a fraud, fear of confrontation and fear of failure. It is not surprising that we get frightened or anxious. Fear is a natural human emotion. However, we can exaggerate the possibility and the severity of a painful outcome and under-estimate our capacity to cope and overcome. So instead of facing our fears, we use one of four avoidance strategies:

- Procrastination (I'll do it but not today or the day after.)
- Excuses (It's not a good idea. It's too dangerous. I didn't want to do it anyway.)
- Distractions (I'd like to do it but actually I'm far too busy.)
- Using other people as shields or props (You do it for me or I'll do if it you come too.)

However, coping strategies make the original problem even worse:

Frightening Situation

↓

Avoidance

↓

Some short-term relief

↓

No chance to test validity of fears

↓

Distortion gets bigger

↓

Long-term fear increases

Understanding how fear feeds on itself helped Margery make significant progress. I also asked her the following questions about her fear of shopping alone. Her answers are in the brackets:

1. What am I afraid of? *(Making a fool of myself.)*
2. Am I exaggerating or distorting the scale of any possible catastrophe? *(The worst that could happen is that I'd need to abandon my trolley and walk out of the store. I doubt anybody would notice or give it even a passing thought.)*

3. What am I losing by not tackling my fears? *(I often spend my day off stuck at home.)*
4. What resources do I have? *(David will help me and so will my son.)*
5. How will I feel once I've faced up to my fears? *(Pretty good.)*

Margery broke her fear of leaving the house on her own into manageable chunks. She walked to the neighbourhood postbox and posted a letter; she walked to and sat in a local park for ten minutes; and she asked David to wait in the car while she started the weekly supermarket shop and then join her after ten minutes.

GRATITUDE DIARY

When life has been difficult, it is easy to become preoccupied with what you are missing and forget about the benefits of what you have. This can lead to unhappiness and even depression. Conversely, if you can keep hold of the positives, you will be more optimistic and more likely to achieve your goals. This is where the gratitude diary comes in.

1. **Buy an attractive notebook.** Find something that is a joy to have by your bed, on your desk or in your briefcase.

2. **Make a contract with yourself to fill it in two or three times a week.** Sunday night when you are looking back over the past week and forward to the next is a good time.

3. **Start each entry with 'Today, I feel grateful for . . .'** Normally these small moments pass us by, but writing them down keeps them fresh and stops us forgetting.

4. **Aim for five items a day.** Find something that came directly out of your recent experiences. For example, 'Someone gave up their seat on the train' or 'I had a call from an old friend'. If you find it hard to come up with five items, go for something enduring like 'The view from my bedroom window' which otherwise you might take for granted.

5. **Think about these five headings.** Friends and family (for example, the enduring support of a sister), work (the chance to travel or meet someone interesting), the wider community (a great delicatessen near where I live), something beautiful or sensual (walking home through the park or the smell of freshly roasted coffee), something

intellectually stimulating (a great debate at the water cooler, an interesting book or great music).

The Bully Trap

Everyone is well aware of the damage done to children by playground bullies. What is less talked about is how adults are bullied too, the impact on their self-esteem and how it can make them fearful on a day-to-day basis.

People generally bully for two reasons. Firstly, they are overworked, stressed and have acted thoughtlessly. Secondly, they have low self-esteem and bully to bolster their status or feel better about themselves. So bullying probably says more about the bully than the bullied. If you find yourself brought down by either type of bully, take a deep breath and act calmly. Tell the person concerned how you feel. Be specific about the behaviour that was unreasonable or unfair but be prepared for them to be dismissive, offhand, puzzled or to use humour to put you down. Bullies are also likely to downgrade your complaint by isolating it to this specific incident. Therefore, be ready with more examples which show the pattern.

If your foe is bullying because of low self-esteem, he or she is unlikely to back down and apologise – or will do so only grudgingly – but do not confuse their reaction with the outcome. Hopefully, the bully will reflect privately on his or her behaviour and be more thoughtful next time round. If not, make a list of future incidents and keep copies of emails or other evidence, and if it is a work situation, complain to a superior. However, be careful not to label fair criticism or justified censure – just because it makes you uncomfortable – as bullying. If your partner is sometimes a bully and even pointing this out makes no impact on his or her behaviour, there is further help in another book in this series: *Help Your Partner Say 'Yes'*.

HOW TO SEEK FEEDBACK

Honest and thoughtful feedback helps you grow and hone your work and relationship skills:

1. **Pick the right person to ask for feedback.**
   This should be someone who is relaxed, knowledgeable and trustworthy. Avoid people who will score points or crow about how much they know.

2. **Prepare your mentor.** On-the-spot advice is likely to be hurried, superficial or not thought out. So make an appointment to talk.

3. **Explain what you need.** Ask for feedback on what you're doing right as well as wrong.

4. **Seek examples.** Rather than accepting blanket statements such as 'You make other people feel small', ask for specific incidents: 'You really exploded when I knocked over your tea.'

5. **Just listen.** Don't explain, offer explanations, justify or defend yourself as this will stop you hearing what is being said. It will also discourage your mentor from being honest next time round.

6. **Thank your mentor and sleep on the advice.** It takes a while to process feedback. Just because your mentor believes something does not necessarily make it true. Only take on board the feedback which chimes with your gut feelings and that *you* believe to be true.

The Mistakes Trap

We all make mistakes. It's another part of being human. However, instead of berating yourself – with *should*, *must*, *never* and *always* – pick one of the following positive ways of talking to yourself:

Specific talk. For example: 'I got off to a bad start because I got lost and arrived late.' This keeps the behaviour isolated to a certain time and place and therefore can be easily fixed (by allowing extra time to find somewhere new).

Situation talk. For example: 'The whole office was on edge because of talk of redundancies.' This points the finger towards a particular set of circumstances – which probably won't be repeated – rather than taking all the blame yourself.

Competent talk. For example: 'I believe in myself' or 'I know how to do this'. This will help remind you of what you did right, rather than focus on what went wrong.

Learning talk. For example: 'That's something I won't do again' or 'It wasn't as bad as I expected'. With this mindset, no experience is ever wasted.

Adopting these positive types of internal dialogue will allow you to acknowledge your mistakes but not lose confidence in your abilities.

The Knock-back Trap

It is inevitable that there will be setbacks on your road to recovery. This is not a reflection on you or your abilities – just a fact of life. What counts is not how bad the knock-back is but your reaction to it. So here are some ways to ensure that you keep moving forward:

- **Remind yourself of your achievements.** These can be lessons learned doing my programme or life achievements to date (such as gaining a degree, a good job or bringing up healthy and happy children).

- **Remember your skills.** Make a list of everything at which you excel and the qualities that other people value or admire. If you can't come up with any ideas, ask a friend or your partner.

- **Accept the compliments.** Most times when someone criticises or points out a mistake, there is normally some positive feedback too. Unfortunately, we often do not hear it or just dismiss it. So hold on to what went right as much as striving to change what went wrong.

- **Stick to your principles.** In many cases, errors or unfortunate outcomes come from us not being true to ourselves. We will agree to doing something that doesn't feel right or back down over something we should have fought for.

- **Look forwards rather than backwards.** After a short post-mortem, so that you can learn from the experience, concentrate on the next challenge. Horse-riding instructors get students back in the saddle as soon as possible after a fall (so that they don't lose their nerve) and set them an easy task (so they feel good about themselves). What goal would work for you?

- **Fake it until you can make it.** Until you are ready to be truly confident again, pretend and behave 'as if' you feel confident. What would you do differently? Why not try it out? Before too long, you'll discover that instead of pretending to have your confidence back – you'll be doing it for real.

When I did this exercise with Margery, she had two stories that illustrated her achievements. She regularly had to cover for a work colleague who, instead of being grateful, would run her down in emails. Instead of getting upset, Margery asked their boss if he was satisfied with her work. 'He was really complimentary, so I showed him the emails and he was most upset. If anything, it was my colleague's work that was not up to standard. He asked if I'd like him to speak with my colleague but I decided it was my problem and I would deal with it. At our regular handover session, I brought the issue up and she apologised. In the past, I would have stewed all weekend or not brought it up at all – but I just thought "I'm in the right" and "I need to stand up for myself".'

Margery had also made progress with her shopping phobia. She was in a department store with David and her mother. He was trying on shoes and she had something to return to another floor; her mother offered to come with her but she decided to go on her own: 'It was only going to take five minutes and I told myself: "You know where they are if you need them" and "I really need to do this". And, of course, I had no problem at all.' When I asked Margery to list her skills, she immediately said bravery and, with a little coaxing, added being a good friend, good wife, mother and daughter.

When I asked about her ambitions for the future, she came up with two realistic goals. First, to make a good female friend. Second, to go out on her own. When she looked back at her skills, she discovered that she already had the necessary qualities: being a good friend and bravery.

Summing Up

Ultimately good self-esteem is built up, day-by-day, through tackling and overcoming obstacles. When mistakes happen, as they will, you have accumulated the tools to recover and carry on without liking or loving yourself any less.

IN A NUTSHELL:

- Don't be afraid to ask for help – especially when dealing with bullying.
- Criticism can be a gift that helps you grow.
- Moving out of your comfort zone and stretching yourself will pay dividends.

FINAL NUTSHELLS

1. Understand the Problem

People are not born with low self-esteem nor do they magically acquire it. The messages from our parents and other significant adults colour our opinion of ourselves.

- We have a legacy not only from each of our parents but also from their relationship with each other.

- If your parents got divorced when you were a child, you will find it especially hard to have a balanced picture of yourself and could feel responsible in some way for the break-up. Needless to say, this is not conducive to building good self-esteem.

- If deep down you consider yourself to be unworthy of love, you will attract partners who will treat you as if you are.

- Self-awareness and self-esteem go hand-in-hand.

Checkpoint: Be more of a friend to yourself. Think of all the qualities that you expect of a good friend. Make a list. Think of the qualities that your friends possess and add those too. I'd be very surprised if your list includes perfection. This is because we are happy to accept our friends, warts and all. If you can do it for a friend, why not for yourself?

2. Let Go of the Past

The past is most likely to ambush us when we close our eyes or downplay its importance. Therefore, facing up to the legacy of our childhood is a vital ingredient for having a better relationship with our parents and ourselves today:

- Although it is important to acknowledge the impact of our parents on our self-esteem, we should not blame them. They, after all, were the products of their own upbringing.

- Our relationship with our father colours our relationship with all the other men we will meet, and our relationship with our mother, with all future women. Unless we make peace with our parents, we risk acting out all our old problems with our partners.

- Give both your mother and father equal parenting rights. This is especially important for children whose parents got divorced. They need to deal with the loss, anger and the fantasy of how things might have been.

- Forgiveness allows you to move on and start afresh.

Checkpoint: Abandon false hopes. Stop thinking that some miracle will happen and change the problems that lie at the root of your low self-esteem. Waiting for other people to apologise or accept what they have done leaves you trapped in the past. Only you are in a position to change your life for the better, so act now and feel empowered.

3. Don't Let Other People Run You Down

Relying on the good opinions of others – or attracting lots of admirers – puts all your self-esteem in their hands:

- Sometimes we hear criticism, even when none is meant, because someone's tone, words or body language triggers particular memories and relationships from the past.

- Check out what was really meant before jumping to negative conclusions.

- If someone has a strong reaction to you, it could be you have hooked into one of their old scripts.

- Constructive criticism could help you learn, improve and ultimately feel better about yourself.

Checkpoint: Harness the power of a fully imagined rehearsal. Imagine yourself with someone who pushes all your wrong buttons and makes you overreact. Imagine that person being irritating. Imagine yourself being calm. How would you stand? How would your body feel? What would you say? What would be your tone of voice? Once you have fully imagined dealing with this difficult person, you are ready to tackle him or her.

4. Reprogramme Your Inner Voice

Inside most people with low self-esteem, there is a small voice which undermines them:

- Most people alternate between allowing their negative voice to rabbit on uninterrupted and trying to ignore it completely.

- Next time, try challenging this voice and asking for evidence of its claims.

- Alternatively, distract your brain and lose the negative voice.

- The brain loves questions – look how many people do crosswords, sudoku and word puzzles on long journeys. So instead of allowing your voice to launch into criticism set it some questions: How could I do this better? Why did that happen? What would happen if I did that?

- Give your brain time to answer, mull over the issues and come back to the question the next day.

- Slowly you will develop a questioning voice (free, open to alternatives and taking its time) which is in direct contrast to the negative voice (closed, certain and quick to reach conclusions).

Checkpoint: Record your progress. Progress is seldom made in huge leaps – which are easy to recognise – but in small victories – which are easy to overlook. So at the end of each week, look back and review often. What have you achieved? What positive messages have you heard from your inner voice? How has this changed your life?

5. Set Realistic Goals

These will support your journey to greater self-belief because there is nothing that boosts confidence more than a job well done.

- Great change is made through small steps over time.

- Unfortunately, we want big changes and overnight.

- This 'I want it all and I want it now' mentality sets up disappointment and risks reconfirming our low opinion of ourselves.

- The biggest problems come from taking short cuts.

- The most progress comes from mapping out a realistic journey and breaking it into small and manageable chunks.

Checkpoint: Reverse the order that you do things. Generally, we put the task we like or find easiest first and put off what we don't like or find easy. In the meantime, this unloved or feared task grows bigger and harder. So put the things you don't like to the top of the list. Not only will you tackle them when you have the most energy but they will also have no time to fester and undermine your belief in yourself.

6. Rebalance Yourself

How you perceive yourself and how you treat yourself are important because this is how other people will perceive and treat you:

- Strive for a balance of head and heart, family and work, valuing yourself and taking into consideration other people's needs.

- In our middle years, when we look back over what we have achieved and forward to what lies ahead, balance is particularly important. So if you have been very work-focused, find other sources of self-worth, and if you have been family orientated, look for a role in the larger world.

- Ultimately success and failure are impostors. By this I mean success is never as wonderful as we expect (and often comes with all sorts of problems) and failure is never as terrible (and many new doors can open from what seem like dead-ends).

- Problems lie in the extremes; look for a solution somewhere in the middle.

Checkpoint: Simplify your lifestyle. Trying to cram too much into a day leaves us exhausted, dissatisfied and critical of ourselves for not pulling off the impossible. Go back through your diary and see if you have a tendency to underestimate time for travelling or completing a task. Have you built in time for hold-ups or setbacks? Could this schedule only work in the best of circumstances? Next think about the activities in your diary. How much pleasure did you get from each event? Was everything strictly necessary? What would have happened if some items had been crossed out? Finally use this knowledge to ensure that you do not over-commit in the future.

7. Conquer Fears and Setbacks

Each day-to-day victory will help cement the internal positive changes from the previous six steps:

- Everybody faces challenges, obstacles and disasters.

- The difference between confident and less confident people is that the former say 'yes' to a new challenge and get a boost from over-coming their fears. When something goes wrong they draw a conclusion that is specific to these circumstances rather than something about their character.

- Taking one risk will make the next risk easier.

- Accept that mistakes happen all the time.

- Even if something goes wrong, you will learn something positive for the future.

- Trust in yourself and embrace life with both hands.

Checkpoint: Encourage others. Helping your family, friends and work colleagues value themselves will help you value yourself too. When someone does something well, make your praise genuine and specific (as this makes it easier to accept). When you have a problem, critique the behaviour not the person. By being positive, you will attract other positive people into your life and boost your overall sense of well-being.

FINAL NUTSHELL:

- Instead of ricocheting between high and low self-esteem, aim to feel good enough about yourself.
- Understand how the past affects today and then forgive your parents and yourself.
- Identify your guardian voice and then nurture it and listen to it.

A Note on the Author

Andrew G. Marshall is a marital therapist and the author of *I Love You But I'm Not In Love With You: Seven Steps to Saving Your Relationship*, *The Single Trap: The Two-step Guide to Escaping It and Finding Lasting Love* and *How Can I Ever Trust You Again?: Infidelity: From Discovery to Recovery in Seven Steps*. He writes for *The Times*, the *Mail on Sunday*, the *Guardian*, *Psychologies* and women's magazines around the world. His work has been translated into over fifteen languages. Andrew trained with RELATE and has a private practice offering counselling, workshops, training days and inspirational talks.

www.andrewgmarshall.com